Y0-CCU-158

DISCARD

SMALL TALK

Western Europe

10
ESSENTIAL
LANGUAGES
FOR
CITY BREAKS

Small Talk Western Europe
1st edition – March 2007

Published by
Lonely Planet Publications Pty Ltd ABN 36 005 607 983
90 Maribyrnong St, Footscray, Victoria 3011, Australia

Lonely Planet Offices
Australia Locked Bag 1, Footscray, Victoria 3011
USA 150 Linden St, Oakland CA 94607
UK 72–82 Rosebery Ave, London, EC1R 4RW

Publishing Manager Chris Rennie
Commissioning Editor Karin Vidstrup Monk
Project Manager Adam McCrow
Series Designer Yukiyoshi Kamimura
Layout Designers David Kemp, Katie Thuy Bui
Editors Branislava Vladisavljevic, Francesca Coles

Cover
Business architecture, Frederic Cirou/Photolibrary; Smiling girl,
Dallas Stribley/Lonely Planet Images; Coffee cup, Richard Nebesky/
Lonely Planet Images

ISBN 978 1 74179 108 2

10 9 8 7 6 5 4 3 2

Printed through Colorcraft Ltd, Hong Kong
Printed in China

Contents

Contents

Italian　63

Portuguese　73

Spanish　83

Swedish　93

Turkish　103

24 hours in the city　113

Index　124

Western Europe – at a glance

Going away for the day, the weekend or the classic short break? *Small Talk Western Europe* gives you the essential language you need to live it up in Western Europe. Get hot tips in our '24 hours in the city' feature and talk your way to the hidden coffee shops in Amsterdam, the boutiques of Paris or a Pilsner in Berlin. Dip into our 'Festivals' feature, get your party shoes on and take part in this exciting region's cultural mayhem.

A bit about the languages … Most of them, including English, belong to the Indo-European language family. Luckily for English speakers, all but one use Roman script. The Romance languages (French, Italian, Spanish and Portuguese) all developed from Vulgar Latin, whereas the Germanic languages (Dutch and German) are more closely related to English. The Scandinavian languages (Danish and Swedish) have developed from Old Norse, the language of the Vikings. Greek, the language of the *Iliad* and the *Odyssey*, forms a separate branch of the Indo-European language family and uses Greek script. Turkish is part of the Ural-Altaic language family, and luckily Arabic script was replaced by Roman script in the early 20th century. Whichever language – this is one region sure to set the senses in overdrive.

did you know?

- The European Union (EU) was established by the Maastricht Treaty in 1992 and developed from the European Economic Community, founded in 1957. Since the 2004 enlargement, it has 27 member states and 23 official languages.
- The euro has been in circulation since 1 January 2002. Its symbol (€) was inspired by the Greek letter epsilon (ε), in recognition of Greece being the cradle of European civilisation.
- The Eurovision Song Contest, held each May, has been running since 1956. For the larger part of the competition's history, the performers were only allowed to sing in their country's national language, but that's no longer the case.

abbreviations

f	feminine	sg	singular	inf	informal
m	masculine	pl	plural	pol	polite

Western Europe

- Danish
- Dutch
- French
- German
- Greek
- Italian
- Portuguese

6

Stockholm

Estonia
Latvia
Lithuania
Kaliningrad
(Russia)
Russia
Russia
Belarus
Poland
Ukraine
Slovakia
Moldova
Sea of
Azov
Hungary
Romania
BLACK SEA
Georgia
Bosnia-
Hercegovina
Serbia
Montenegro
Bulgaria
Armenia
FYROM
Istanbul
Ankara
TURKEY
Albania
Thessaloniki
Aegean
Sea
GREECE
Izmir
Ionian
Sea
Athens
Nicosia
(Lefkosia)
Syria
SEA
Sea of Crete
CYPRUS
Lebanon
Crete
Iraq

Spanish
Swedish
Turkish
Note: Language areas are
approximate only.

7

EUROPE

January

Camel Wrestling Championship	**Turkey**	
Carnival season	**Germany**	Jan/Feb
Epiphany (Blessing of the Waters)	**Greece**	6th
International Circus Festival of Monte Carlo	**France**	
La Tamborrada (street drumming parades)	**Spain**	20th
New Year's Day Concert in Vienna	**Austria**	1st

February

Berlin International Film Festival	**Germany**	
Copenhagen International Fashion Fair	**Denmark**	
March of the Gilles (orange-throwing festival)	**Belgium**	Feb/Mar
Masked Carnival in Venice	**Italy**	

March

Festival of Snakes	**Italy**	19th
Holy Week	**Portugal**	Mar/Apr
Las Fallas Fire Festival	**Spain**	15th–19th

April

Feria de Abril (April Fair)	**Spain**	
Maggio Musicale Fiorentino (festival of opera, ballet and concerts)	**Italy**	Apr–Jun
Queen's Day	**The Netherlands**	30th

May

Brussels Jazz Marathon	**Belgium**	
Cannes Film Festival	**France**	17th–28th
Festival of Cats	**Belgium**	
Gypsy Pilgrimage (with music and feasting)	**France**	
Wave-Gotik-Treffen Festival (gathering of 20,000 Goths)	**Germany**	May/Jun

June

Amsterdam Roots Festival (world music and culture)	**The Netherlands**	
The Baby-Jumping Colacho Festival (Corpus Christi celebration)	**Spain**	
Bordeaux Wine Festival	**France**	Jun–Jul
Carnival of Cultures (ethnic communities festival)	**Germany**	
Festa do Santo Antonio (celebration of the 'saint of love')	**Portugal**	13th
Festival Couleur Café (world music festival)	**Belgium**	Jun–Jul
Festival of the Flood (water sports and partying)	**Cyprus**	
Hellenic Festival	**Greece**	
Kirkpinar Oil Wrestling	**Turkey**	late Jun
La Battala dos Vinos (War of the Wines)	**Spain**	29th
Midsummer's Eve	**Denmark**	late Jun
Spoleto Festival (performing arts festival)	**Italy**	Jun–Jul

July

Bastille Day	**France**	14th
Berlin Love Parade (techno party)	**Germany**	
Copenhagen Jazz Festival	**Denmark**	
Festival of the Giants (parade of giant figures)	**France**	
Il Palio (horse race in Siena)	**Italy**	Jul/Aug
Nice Jazz Festival	**France**	
Roskilde Festival (outdoor music festival)	**Denmark**	
Salzburger Festspiele (music and drama festival)	**Austria**	
San Fermín (Running of the Bulls)	**Spain**	
Stockholm Pride Festival (gay community festival)	**Sweden**	Jul/Aug
Tour de France	**France**	
Wagner Festival (opera)	**Germany**	Jul/Aug
World Bodypainting Festival	**Austria**	

August

Festival of Ancient Drama	**Greece**	Aug/Sep
La Tomatina (tomato-throwing festival)	**Spain**	last Wed
Samothraki Dance Festival (electronic music festival)	**Greece**	
Schueberfouer (Funfair)	**Luxembourg**	Aug/Sep
Venice International Film Festival	**Italy**	end Aug
Zurich Street Parade (techno party)	**Switzerland**	

September

Århus Festival (arts and culture festival)	**Denmark**	
Feria du Riz (rice festival)	**France**	mid Sep
Lemesos Wine Festival	**Cyprus**	30th–11th

October

Oktoberfest (beer festival)	**Germany**	late Sep/ early Oct

November

Amsterdam *Sinterklaas* Procession (Santa Claus parade)	**The Netherlands**	
High Times Cannabis Cup (marijuana festival)	**The Netherlands**	late Nov
Potsdamer Platz Winter Sledging	**Germany**	
Stockholm International Film Festival	**Sweden**	
Tivoli's Christmas Markets	**Denmark**	Nov/Dec

December

Africolor (world theatre and music festival)	**France**	
The Cresta Run (a 1200-yard toboggan ice run)	**Switzerland**	Dec–Mar
Christmas Beer Festival	**Belgium**	
Christmas Festival in Catalonia	**Spain**	
Festival of the Whirling Dervishes	**Turkey**	
Kaiserball (Imperial Ball)	**Austria**	31st
The Paris Parade Festival	**France**	Dec–Jan

Festivals

Public holidays

New Year's Day	1 January
Greek Independence Day (Greece)	25 March
Independence/Children's Day (Turkey)	23 April
Liberty Day (Portugal)	25 April
Queen's Day (The Netherlands)	30 April
May (Labour) Day (all except The Netherlands & Turkey)	1 May
Common Prayer Day (Denmark)	fourth Friday after Easter
Whitmonday (Denmark, Germany, The Netherlands, Sweden)	eighth Monday after Easter
Midsummer's Day (Sweden)	first Saturday after 21 June
Bastille Day (France)	14 July
Feast of the Assumption (France, Italy, Portugal, Spain)	15 August
Day of German Unity (Germany)	3 October
National Day (Spain)	12 October
Ohi Day (Greece)	28 October
Anniversary of Ataturk's Death (Turkey)	10 November
All Saints' Day (Italy, Portugal, Spain, Sweden)	early November
Christmas Day (all except Turkey)	25 December
Second Day of Christmas (Denmark, Greece, The Netherlands, Sweden)	26 December
St Stephen's Day (Italy)	26 December

Danish

In Denmark, every corner of the country is in on the party.

Pronunciation

Vowels		Consonants	
Symbol	English sound	Symbol	English sound
a	act	b	bed
aa	father	ch	cheat
ai	aisle	d	dog
aw	saw	dh	that
e	bet	f	fat
ee	see	g	go
eu	nurse	h	hat
ew	ee pronounced with rounded lips	j	joke
ey	as in 'bet', but longer	k	kit
i	hit	l	lot
o	pot	m	man
oh	note	n	not
oo	soon	ng	ring
ow	how	p	pet
oy	toy	r	red (trilled)
		s	sun
		sh	shot
		t	top
		v	very
		w	win
		y	yellow

The Danish pronunciation is given in blue after each word or phrase. Read these words as though you were reading English and you're sure to be understood. Each syllable is separated by a dot, and italics indicate that you need to put stress on that syllable, for example:

Undskyld. awn·skewl

essentials

Yes/No.	*Ja/Nej.*	ya/nai
Hello/Goodbye.	*Hej/Farvel.*	hai/faar·*vel*
Please.	*Vær så venlig.*	ver saw *ven*·lee
Thank you (very much).	*(Mange) Tak.*	(*mang*·e) taak
You're welcome.	*Selv tak.*	sel taak
Excuse me.	*Undskyld mig.*	*awn*·skewl mai
Sorry.	*Undskyld.*	*awn*·skewl

Do you speak English?
Taler De/du engelsk? pol/inf   ta·la dee/doo *eng*·elsk

Do you understand?
Forstår De/du? pol/inf   for·*stawr* dee/doo

I (don't) understand.
Jeg forstår (ikke).   yai for·*stawr* (*i*·ke)

chatting

introductions

Mr	*Hr*	heyr
Mrs/Miss	*Fru/Frøken*	froo/*freu*·ken
How are you?	*Hvordan går det?*	vor·*dan* gawr dey
Well, thanks.	*Godt, tak.*	got taak
What's your name?	*Hvad hedder De/du?* pol/inf	va *hey*·dha dee/doo
My name is ...	*Mit navn er ...*	mit nown ir ...
I'm pleased to meet you.	*Hyggeligt at møde Dem/dig.* pol/inf	*hew*·ge·leet at *meu*·dhe dem/dai

Here's my (email) address.
Her er min (email) adresse.   heyr ir meen (*ee*·mayl) a·*draa*·se

What's your (email) address?
Hvad er Deres/din (email) adresse? pol/inf   va ir *de*·res/deen (*ee*·mayl) a·*draa*·se

15

Here's my phone number.
Her er mit telefonnummer. heyr ir meet tey·ley·*fohn*·naw·ma

What's your phone number?
Hvad er Deres/dit va ir *de*·res/deet
telefonnummer? pol/inf tey·ley·*fohn*·naw·ma

What's your occupation?
Hvad laver De/du? pol/inf va *la*·va dee/doo

I'm a ...	*Jeg er ...*	yai ir ...
businessperson	*forretnings-*	for·*rat*·nings·
	drivende	dree·ve·ne
student	*studerende*	stoo·*dey*·re·ne

Where are you from?
Hvor kommer De/du fra? pol/inf vor *ko*·ma dee/doo fraa

I'm from (England).
Jeg er fra (England). yai ir fraa (*eng*·lan)

Are you married?
Er De/du gift? pol/inf ir dee/doo geeft

I'm married/single.
Jeg er gift/ugift. yai ir geeft/*oo*·geeft

How old are you?
Hvor gammel er? vor *gaa*·mel ir

I'm ... years old.
Jeg er ... år gammel. yai ir ... awr *gaa*·mel

making conversation

What's the weather like?
Hvordan er vejret? vor·*dan* ir *vey*·ret

It's cold.	*Det er koldt.*	dey ir kolt
It's hot.	*Det er varmt.*	dey ir vaarmt
It's raining.	*Det regner.*	dey *rain*·a
It's snowing.	*Det sner.*	dey sneyr

Do you live here?	*Bor De/du her?* pol/inf	bohr dee/doo heyr
Where are you going?	*Hvor skal De/du hen?* pol/inf	vor skal dee/doo hen
What are you doing?	*Hvad laver De/du?* pol/inf	va *la*·va dee/doo

invitations

Would you like to go (for a) ...?	*Har De/du lyst til ...?* pol/inf	haar dee/doo lewst til ...
dancing	*at tage ud og danse*	at taa oodh o *dan*·se
drink	*en drink*	in drink
meal	*at tage ud og spise*	at ta oodh o *spee*·se
out	*at gå ud*	at gaw oodh

Yes, I'd love to.
Ja, det vil jeg meget gerne.   ya dey vil yai *maa*·yet *gir*·ne

No, I'm afraid I can't.
Nej, det kan jeg desværre ikke.   nai dey kan yai dey·*sve*·re *i*·ke

I love it here!
Her er skønt!
heyr ir skeunt

What time will we meet?
Hvornår skal vi mødes?   vor·*nawr* skal vee *meu*·dhes

Where will we meet?
Hvor skal vi mødes?   vor skal vee *meu*·dhes

Let's meet at ...	*Lad os mødes ...*	ladh os *meu*·dhes ...
(eight) o'clock	*klokken (otte)*	*klo*·ken (*aw*·te)
the entrance	*ved indgangen*	vi *in*·gaang·en

meeting up

Can I ...?	*Må jeg ...?*	maw yai ...
dance with you	*danse med dig*	*dan*·se me dai
sit here	*sidde her*	*si*·dha heyr
take you home	*tage med dig hjem*	ta me dai jem

I'm here with my girlfriend/boyfriend.
Jeg er her med min kæreste.   yai ir heyr me meen *ker*·ste

Keep in touch!
Skriv til mig!   skreev til mai

It's been great meeting you.
Det har været fantastisk   dey haar *ve*·ret fan·*tas*·teesk
at møde Dem/dig. pol/inf   at *meu*·dhe dem/dai

likes & dislikes

I thought it was ...	*Jeg synes det var ...*	yai sewns dey vaar ...
It's ...	*Det er ...*	dey ir ...
awful	*hæsligt*	*hes*·leet
great	*fantastisk*	fan·*tas*·teesk
interesting	*interessant*	in·traa·*sant*
Do you like ...?	*Kan De/du*	kan dee/doo
	lide ...? pol/inf	lee ...
I (don't) like ...	*Jeg synes (ikke)*	yai sewns (*i*·ke)
	om ...	om ...
art	*kunst*	kawnst
shopping	*at handle*	at *han*·le
sport	*sport*	sport

eating & drinking

I'd like ...,	*Jeg vil gerne ...,*	yai vil *gir*·ne ...
please.	*tak.*	taak
a table for	*have et bord til*	ha it bohr til
(four)	*(fire)*	(feer)
the nonsmoking	*sidde i ikke-*	*si*·dha ee *i*·ke·
section	*rygerafdelingen*	*rew*·a·ow·*dey*·ling·en
the smoking	*sidde i*	*si*·dha ee
section	*rygerafdelingen*	*rew*·a·ow·*dey*·ling·en

Do you have vegetarian food?
Har I vegetarmad?   haar ee vey·ge·*taar*·madh

What would you recommend?
Hvad kan De/du anbefale? pol/inf   va kan dee/doo *an*·bey·fa·le

I'll have a ...	*..., tak.*	... taak
Cheers!	*Skål!*	skawl

I'd like (the) ..., please.	Jeg vil gerne have ...	yai vil gir·ne ha ...
bill	regningen	rai·ning·en
drink list	vinkortet	veen·kor·tet
menu	menuen	me·new·en
that dish	den ret	den ret

Would you like a drink?
Vil du have en drink?
vil doo haa in drink

(cup of) coffee/tea	(en kop) kaffe/te	(in kop) ka·fe/tey
(mineral) water	(mineral) vand	(mee·ne·ral) van
bottle of (beer)	en flaske (øl)	in flas·ke (eul)
glass of (wine)	et glas (vin)	it glas (veen)
breakfast	morgenmad	morn·madh
lunch	frokost	froh·kost
dinner	middag	mi·da

exploring

Where's the ...?	Hvor er ...?	vor ir ...
bank	der en bank	deyr in baank
hotel	der et hotel	deyr it hoh·tel
post office	der et postkontor	deyr it post·kon·tohr

Can you show me (on the map)?
Kan De/du vise mig det (på kortet)? pol/inf
kan dee/doo vee·se mai dey (paw kor·tet)

What time does it open/close?
Hvornår åbner/lukker de?
vor·nawr awb·na/law·ka dey

What's the admission charge?
Hvad koster adgang?
va kos·ta adh·gaang

When's the next tour?
Hvornår er den næste tur?
vor·nawr ir den nes·te toor

Where can I find ...?	Hvor kan jeg finde ...?	vor kan yai fi·ne ...
clubs	natklubber	nat·kloo·ba
gay venues	bøsseklubber	beu·se·kloo·ba
pubs	pubber	paw·ba

Can we get there by public transport?

Kan vi tage offentlig transport dertil?	kan vee ta o·fen·lee traans·port deyr·til

Where can I buy a ticket?

Hvor kan jeg købe en billet?	vor ka yai keu·be in bi·let

One ... ticket (to Odense), please.	En ... billet (til Odense), tak.	in ... bee·let (til oh·dhen·se) taak
one-way	enkelt	eng·kelt
return	retur	rey·toor

My luggage has been ...	Min bagage er blevet ...	meen ba·gaa·she ir bley·vet ...
lost	væk	vek
stolen	stjålet	styaw·let

Is this the ... to (Aarhus)?	Er dette ... til (Århus)?	ir dey·te ... til (awr·hoos)
boat	båden	baw·dhen
bus	bussen	boo·sen
plane	flyet	flew·et
train	toget	taw·et

What time's the ... bus?	Hvad tid er den ... bus?	va teedh ir den ... boos
first	første	feurs·te
next	næste	nes·te
last	sidste	sees·te

I'd like a taxi ...	Jeg vil gerne have en taxa ...	yai vil gir·ne ha in tak·sa ...
at (9am)	klokken (ni om morgenen)	klo·ken (nee om mor·nen)
tomorrow	i morgen	ee morn

How much is it to ...?

Hvad koster det at køre til ...?	va kos·ta dey at keu·re til ...

Please take me to (this address).
Vær venlig at køre   ver *ven*·lee at *keu*·re
mig til (denne adresse).   mai til (*de*·ne a·*draa*·se)

Please stop here.
Venligst stop her.   *ven*·leest stop heyr

shopping

Where's	*Hvor er der*	vor ir deyr
(the market)?	*(et marked)?*	(it *maar*·kedh)
I'm looking for ...	*Jeg leder efter ...*	yai *li*·dha *ef*·ta ...
It's faulty.	*Det er i stykker.*	dey ir ee *stew*·ka
I'd like ...,	*Jeg vil gerne have*	yai vil *gir*·ne ha
please.	*..., tak.*	... taak
a refund	*en efundering*	in re·fawn·*dey*·ring
to return this	*returnere dette*	rey·toor·*ney*·re *dey*·te

How much is it?
Hvor meget koster det?   vor *maa*·yet *kos*·ta dey

Can you write down the price?
Kan De/du skrive   ka dee/doo *skree*·ve
prisen ned? pol/inf   *pree*·sen nidh

That's too expensive.
Det er for dyrt.   dey ir for dewrt

There's a mistake in the bill.
Der er en fejl i kvitteringen.   deyr ir in fail ee kvee·*tey*·ring·en

I need a film for this camera.
Jeg har brug for film   yai haar broo for feelm
til dette kamera.   til *dey*·te *ka*·me·raa

Do you accept ...?	*Tager I ...?*	ta ee ...
credit cards	*kreditkort*	kre·*deet*·kort
travellers cheques	*rejsechecks*	*rai*·se·sheks
I'd like ...,	*Jeg vil gerne have*	yai vil *gir*·ne ha
please.	*..., tak.*	... taak
a receipt	*en kvittering*	in kvee·*tey*·ring
my change	*mine byttepenge*	*mee*·ne *bew*·te·peng·e

working

Where's the (business centre)?
Hvor er (forretningscenteret)?   vor ir (for·ret·nings·sen·tredh)

I'm attending a ...   *Jeg er ...*   yai ir ...
  conference   *til konference*   til kon·fe·*rang*·se
  course   *på kursus*   paw *koor*·soos
  meeting   *til møde*   til *meu*·dhe

I'm visiting a trade fair.
Jeg er til handelsmesse.   yai ir til *han*·els·me·se

I have an appointment with ...
Jeg har en aftale med ...   yai haar in *ow*·ta·la me ...

I'm with my colleagues.
Jeg er her med mine kolleger.   yai ir heyr me *mee*·ne koh·*ley*·a

Here's my business card.
Her er mit kort.   heyr ir meet kort

That went very well.
Det gik rigtigt godt.   det geek *rig*·tee got

emergencies

Help!	*Hjælp!*	yelp
Stop!	*Stop!*	stop
Go away!	*Gå væk!*	gaw vek
Thief!	*Tyv!*	tew
Fire!	*Ildebrand!*	*ee*·le·braan

Call ...!   *Ring efter ...!*   ring *ef*·ta ...
  an ambulance   *en ambulance*   in aam·boo·*laang*·se
  a doctor   *en læge*   in *le*·ye
  the police   *politiet*   poh·lee·*tee*·et

Could you help me, please?   *Kan De/du hjælpe mig?* pol/inf   kan dee/doo *yel*·pe mai

I'm lost.   *Jeg er faret vild.*   yai ir *faa*·ret veel

Where's the toilet?   *Hvor er toilettet?*   vor ir toy·*le*·tet

Dutch

> God created the world, but the Dutch
> created the Netherlands.

Pronunciation

Vowels		Consonants	
Symbol	English sound	Symbol	English sound
a	run	b	bed
aa	father	ch	cheat
aw	saw	d	dog
e	bet	f	fat
ee	see	g	go
eu	nurse	h	hat
ew	ee pronounced with rounded lips	k	kit
ey	as in 'bet', but longer	kh	as in Scottish 'loch'
i	hit	l	lot
o	pot	m	man
oh	note	n	not
oo	zoo	ng	ring
öy	her year (without the 'r')	p	pet
u	put	r	red (trilled)
uh	ago	s	sun

The Dutch pronunciation is given in blue after each word or phrase. Read these words as though you were reading English and you're sure to be understood. Each syllable is separated by a dot, and italics indicate that you need to put stress on that syllable, for example:

Pardon.   par·*don*

sh	shot
t	top
v	very
w	win
y	yes
z	zero
zh	pleasure

Dutch

essentials

Yes/No.	*Ja/Nee.*	yaa/ney
Hello/Goodbye.	*Goedendag./Dag.*	khoo·duh·*dakh*/dakh
Please.	*Alstublieft.* pol	al·stew·*bleeft*
	Alsjeblieft. inf	a·shuh·*bleeft*
Thank you	*Dank u (wel).* pol	dangk ew (wel)
(very much).	*Dank je (wel).* inf	dangk yuh (wel)
You're welcome.	*Graag gedaan.*	khraakh khuh·*daan*
Excuse me.	*Pardon.*	par·*don*
Sorry.	*Sorry.*	so·ree

Do you speak English?
Spreekt u Engels? — spreykt ew *eng*·uhls

Do you understand?
Begrijpt u? — buh·*khreypt* ew

I (don't) understand.
Ik begrijp het (niet). — ik buh·*khreyp* huht (neet)

chatting

introductions

Mr	*Meneer*	muh·*neyr*
Mrs/Miss	*Mevrouw/Juffrouw*	muh·*vraw*/yu·fraw
How are you?	*Hoe gaat het met u/jou?* pol/inf	hoo khaat huht met ew/yaw
Fine. And you?	*Goed. En met u/jou?* pol/inf	khoot en met ew/yaw
What's your name?	*Hoe heet u/je?* pol/inf	hoo heyt ew/yuh
My name is ...	*Ik heet ...*	ik heyt ...
I'm pleased to meet you.	*Aangenaam.*	*aan*·khuh·naam
Here's my ...	*Dit is mijn ...*	dit is meyn ...
What's your ...?	*Wat is uw ...?*	wat is ew ...
(email) address	*(e-mail)adres*	(ee·meyl·)a·*dres*
phone number	*telefoonnummer*	tey·ley·*foh*·nu·muhr

What's your occupation?
Wat is uw beroep?   wat is ew buh-*roop*

I'm a ...   *Ik ben ...*   ik ben ...
   businessperson   *zakenman* m   *zaa*-kuh-man
                 zakenvrouw f   *zaa*-kuh-vraw
   student   *student*   stew-*dent*

Where are you from?
Waar komt u vandaan?   waar komt ew van-*daan*
I'm from (England).
Ik kom uit (Engeland).   ik kom öyt (*eng*-uh-lant)
Are you married?
Bent u getrouwd?   bent ew khuh-*trawt*
I'm married/single.
Ik ben getrouwd/vrijgezel.   ik ben khuh-*trawt*/*vrey*-khuh-zel
How old are you?
Hoe oud bent u?   hoo awt bent ew
I'm ... years old.
Ik ben ... jaar.   ik ben ... yaar

making conversation

What's the weather like?
Hoe is het weer?   hoo is huht weyr

It's ...
   cold   *Het is koud.*   huht is kawt
   hot   *Het is zeer warm.*   huht is zeyr warm
   raining   *Het regent.*   huht *rey*-khuhnt
   snowing   *Het sneeuwt.*   huht sneywt

Do you live here?
Woont u hier?   wohnt ew heer
Where are you going?
Waar gaat u heen?   waar khaat ew heyn
What are you doing?
Wat bent u aan het doen?   wat bent ew aan huht doon

Dutch

26

invitations

Would you like to go for a ...?	Heb je zin in een ...?	hep yuh zin in uhn ...
drink	*drankje*	*drangk*·yuh
meal	*maaltijd*	*maal*·teyt

Would you like to go ...?	Heb je zin om ...?	hep yuh zin om ...
dancing	*te gaan dansen*	tuh khaan *dan*·suhn
out	*uit te gaan*	öyt tuh khaan

Yes, I'd love to.
Ja, graag. yaa khraakh

No, I'm afraid I can't.
Nee, ik vrees dat ik niet kan. ney ik freys dat ik neet kan

I love it here!
Ik vind het hier erg leuk!
ik vint huht heer erkh leuk

What time will we meet?
Hoe laat spreken we af? hoo laat *sprey*·kuhn wuh af

Where will we meet?
Waar spreken we af? waar *sprey*·kuhn wuh af

Let's meet at ...	We zien elkaar ...	wuh zeen el·*kaar* ...
(eight) o'clock	*om (acht) uur*	om (akht) ewr
the entrance	*bij de ingang*	bey duh *in*·khang

meeting up

Can I ...?	Mag ik ...?	makh ik ...
dance with you	*met je dansen*	met yuh *dan*·suhn
sit here	*hier zitten*	heer *zi*·tuhn
take you home	*je naar huis vergezellen*	yuh naar höys vuhr·khuh·*ze*·luhn

27

I'm here with my girlfriend/boyfriend.
Ik ben hier met mijn   ik ben heer met meyn
vriendin/vriend.   vreen·*din*/vreent

Keep in touch!
Laat iets van je horen!   laat eets van yuh *hoh*·ruhn

It's been great meeting you.
Het was leuk je te leren   huht was löyk yuh tuh *ley*·ruhn
kennen.   ke·nuhn

likes & dislikes

I thought it was ...	Ik vond het ...	ik vont huht ...
It's ...	Het is ...	huht is ...
awful	afschuwelijk	af·*skhew*·wuh·luhk
great	geweldig	khuh·*wel*·dikh
interesting	interessant	in·tey·rey·*sant*
Do you like ...?	Hou je van ...?	haw yuh van ...
I (don't) like ...	Ik hou (niet) van ...	ik haw (neet) van ...
art	kunst	kunst
shopping	winkelen	*wing*·kuh·luhn
sport	sport	sport

eating & drinking

I'd like ..., please.	Ik wil graag ...	ik wil khraakh ...
a table for (four)	een tafel voor (vier)	uhn *taa*·fuhl vohr (veer)
the (non)smoking section	(niet-)roken	(*neet*·)roh·kuhn

Do you have vegetarian food?
Heeft u vegetarische   heyft ew vey·khey·*taa*·ri·suh
maaltijden?   maal·tey·duhn

What would you recommend?
Wat kunt u aanbevelen?   wat kunt ew *aan*·buh·vey·luhn

I'll have a ...	Voor mij ...	vohr mey ...
Cheers!	Proost!	prohst

Dutch

I'd like (the) ..., please.	..., graag.	... khraakh
bill	De rekening	duh rey-kuh-ning
drink list	De drankkaart	duh drang-kaart
menu	De menu	duh muh-new
that dish	Dat gerecht	dat guh-rekht
(cup of) coffee/tea	(een tas) koffie/thee	(uhn tas) ko-fee/tey
(mineral) water	(mineraal) water	(mee-ney-raal-) waa-tuhr
bottle of (beer)	een flesje (bier)	uhn fle-shuh (beer)
glass of (wine)	een glas (wijn)	uhn khlas (weyn)
breakfast	ontbijt	ont-beyt
lunch	middageten/lunch	mi-dakh-ey-tuhn/lunsh
dinner	avondeten	aa-vont-ey-tuhn

Would you like a drink?
Wil je iets drinken?
wil yuh eets *dring*-kuhn

exploring

Where's the ...?	Waar is ...?	waar is ...
bank	de bank	duh bangk
hotel	het hotel	huht hoh-tel
post office	het postkantoor	huht post-kan-tohr

Can you show me (on the map)?
Kunt u het aanwijzen (op de kaart)?
kunt ew huht *aan*-wey-zuhn (op duh kaart)

What time does it open/close?
Hoe laat gaat het open/dicht?
hoo laat khaat huht *oh*-puhn/dikht

What's the admission charge?
Wat is de toegangsprijs?
wat is duh *too*-khangs-preys

When's the next tour?
Wanneer is de volgende rondleiding?
wa-*neyr* is duh *vol*-khuhn-duh *ront*-ley-ding

29

Where can I find ...?	*Waar vind ik de ...?*	waar vint ik duh ...
clubs	*clubs*	klups
gay venues	*homotenten*	hoh·moh·ten·tuhn
pubs	*kroegen*	khroo·khuhn

Can we get there by public transport?

Kunnen we er met het	ku·nuhn wuh uhr met huht
openbaar vervoer heen?	oh·puhn·baar vuhr·voor heyn

Where can I buy a ticket?

Waar kan ik een	waar kan ik uhn
kaartje kopen?	kaar·chuh koh·puhn

My luggage has been ...	*Mijn bagage is ...*	meyn ba·khaa·zhuh is ...
lost	*verloren*	vuhr·loh·ruhn
stolen	*gestolen*	khuh·stoh·luhn

One ... (to Antwerp), please.	*Een ... (naar Antwerpen) graag.*	uhn ... (naar ant·wer·puhn) khraakh
one-way ticket	*enkele reis*	eng·kuh·luh reys
return ticket	*retourtje*	ruh·toor·chuh

Is this the ... to (Amsterdam)?	*Is dit ... naar (Amsterdam)?*	is dit ... naar (am·stuhr·dam)
boat	*de boot*	duh boht
bus	*de bus*	duh bus
plane	*het vliegtuig*	huht vleekh·töykh
train	*de trein*	duh treyn

What time's the ... bus?	*Hoe laat gaat de ... bus?*	hoo laat khaat duh ... bus
first	*eerste*	eyr·stuh
last	*laatste*	laat·stuh
next	*volgende*	vol·khuhn·duh

I'd like a taxi ...	*Ik wil graag een taxi ...*	ik wil khraakh uhn tak·see ...
at (9am)	*om (negen uur 's ochtends)*	om (ney·khuhn ewr sokh·tuhns)
tomorrow	*voor morgen*	vohr mor·khuhn

How much is it to …?
Hoeveel kost het naar …?   hoo·*veyl* kost huht naar …

Please take me to (this address).
Breng me alstublieft naar   breng muh al·stew·*bleeft* naar
(dit adres).   (dit a·*dres*)

Please stop here.
Stop hier alstublieft.   stop heer al·stew·*bleeft*

shopping

Where's	*Waar is*	waar is
(the market)?	*(de markt)?*	(duh mart)
I'm looking for …	*Ik ben op zoek naar …*	ik ben op zook naar …
It's faulty.	*Het werkt niet.*	huht werkt neet
I'd like …, please.	*Ik wil graag …*	ik wil khraakh …
a refund	*mijn geld terug*	meyn gelt tuh·*rukh*
to return this	*dit retourneren*	dit ruh·toor·*ney*·ruhn

How much is it?
Hoeveel kost het?   hoo·*veyl* kost huht

That's too expensive.
Dat is te duur.   dat is tuh dewr

Can you write down the price?
Kunt u de prijs   kunt ew duh preys
opschrijven?   op·*skhrey*·vuhn

There's a mistake in the bill.
Er zit een fout in de rekening.   uhr zit uhn fawt in duh *rey*·kuh·ning

I need a film for this camera.
Ik heb een film nodig   ik hep uhn film *noh*·dikh …
voor dit fototoestel.   vohr dit *foh*·toh·too·stel

Do you accept …?	*Accepteert u …?*	ak·sep·*teyrt* ew …
credit cards	*kredietkaarten*	krey·*deet*·kaar·tuhn
travellers cheques	*reischeques*	*reys*·sheks
I'd like …, please.	*Ik wil graag …*	ik wil khraakh …
a receipt	*een kwitantie*	uhn kwee·*tan*·see
my change	*mijn wisselgeld*	meyn *wi*·suhl·gelt

31

working

I'm attending a ...	Ik neem deel aan een ...	ik neym deyl aan uhn ...
conference	conferentie	kon·fey·ren·see
course	opleiding	op·ley·ding
meeting	vergadering	vuhr·khaa·duh·ring

Where's the (business centre)?
Waar is (het zakencentrum)? waar is (huht *zaa*·kuhn·sen·truhm)

I'm visiting a trade fair.
Ik ga naar een beurs. ik khaa naar uhn beurs

I have an appointment with ...
Ik heb een afspraak met ... ik hep uhn *af*·spraak met ...

I'm with my colleagues.
Ik ben hier met collega's. ik ben heer met koh·*ley*·khas

Here's my business card.
Hier is mijn visitekaartje. heer is meyn vee·*see*·tuh·kaar·chuh

That went very well.
Dat ging vlotjes. dat khing *vlot*·yuhs

emergencies

Help!	Help!	help
Stop!	Stop!	stop
Go away!	Ga weg!	khaa wekh
Thief!	Dief!	deef
Fire!	Brand!	brant

Call ...!	Bel ...!	bel ...
an ambulance	een ambulance	uhn am·bew·*lans*
a doctor	een doktor	uhn *dok*·tuhr
the police	de politie	duh poh·*leet*·see

Could you help me, please?
Kunt u mij alstublieft helpen? kunt ew mey al·stew·*bleeft hel*·puhn

I'm lost.
Ik ben de weg kwijt. ik ben duh wekh kweyt

Where are the toilets?
Waar zijn de toiletten? waar zeyn duh twa·*le*·tuhn

French

> Paris is the Paris of Parisians, the Paris of France, the one and only Paris. Nothing comes close.

Pronunciation

Vowels		Consonants	
Symbol	English sound	Symbol	English sound
a	run	b	bed
ai	aisle	d	dog
air	fair	f	fat
e	bet	g	go
ee	see	k	kit
eu	nurse	l	lot
ew	ee pronounced with rounded lips	m	man
ey	as in 'bet', but longer	n	not
o	pot	ny	canyon
oo	moon	ng	ring
om/on/ong	like the 'o' in 'pot', plus nasal consonant sound	p	pet
um/un/ung	similar to the 'a' in 'bat', plus nasal consonant sound	r	run (throaty)
The French pronunciation is given in blue after each word or phrase. Read these words as though you were reading English and you're sure to be understood. Each syllable is separated with a dot, for example:		s	sun
		sh	shot
		t	top
		v	very
		w	win
Merci. mair·see		y	yes
		z	zero
		zh	pleasure

French

essentials

Yes/No.	*Oui/Non.*	wee/non
Hello/Goodbye.	*Bonjour/Au revoir.*	bon·zhoor/o re·vwar
Please.	*S'il vous plaît.*	seel voo pley
Thank you (very much).	*Merci (beaucoup).*	mair·see (bo·koo)
You're welcome.	*Je vous en prie.*	zhe voo zon·pree
Excuse me.	*Excusez-moi.*	ek·skew·zey·mwa
Sorry.	*Pardon.*	par·don

Do you speak English?
   Parlez-vous anglais?   par·ley·voo ong·gley

Do you understand?
   Comprenez-vous?   kom·pre·ney·voo

I understand.
   Je comprends.   zhe kom·pron

I don't understand.
   Je ne comprends pas.   zhe ne kom·pron pa

chatting

French

introductions

Mr	*Monsieur*	me·syeu
Mrs	*Madame*	ma·dam
Miss	*Mademoiselle*	mad·mwa·zel
How are you?	*Comment allez-vous?*	ko·mon ta·ley·voo
Fine, thanks.	*Bien, merci.*	byun mair·see
And you?	*Et vous?*	ey voo
What's your name?	*Comment vous appelez-vous?*	ko·mon voo za·pley·voo
My name is ...	*Je m'appelle ...*	zhe ma·pel ...
I'm pleased to meet you.	*Enchanté.* m *Enchantée.* f	on·shon·tey on·shon·tey

35

Here's my ...	Voici mon ...	vwa·see mon ...
What's your ...?	Quel est votre ...?	kel ey vo·tre ...
(email) address	(e-mail) adresse	(ey·mel) a·dress
phone number	numéro de	new·mey·ro de
	téléphone	tey·ley·fon

What's your occupation?
Vous faites quoi comme métier?   voo fet kwa kom mey·tyey

I'm a ...	Je suis un/une ... m/f	zhe swee zun/zewn ...
businessperson	homme/femme	om/fem
	d'affaires m/f	da·fair
student	étudiant m	ey·tew·dyon
	étudiante f	ey·tew·dyont

Where are you from?
Vous venez d'où?   voo ve·ney doo

I'm from (England).
Je viens (d'Angleterre).   zhe vyun (dong·gle·tair)

Are you married?
Est-ce que vous êtes marié(e)? m/f   es·ke voo zet mar·yey

I'm married.
Je suis marié(e). m/f   zhe swee mar·yey

I'm single.
Je suis célibataire. m&f   zhe swee sey·lee·ba·tair

How old are you?
Quel âge avez-vous?   kel azh a·vey·voo

I'm ... years old.
J'ai ... ans.   zhey ... on

making conversation

What's the weather like?
Quel temps fait-il?   kel tom fey·teel

It's ...		
cold	Il fait froid.	eel fey frwa
hot	Il fait chaud.	eel fey sho
raining	Il pleut.	eel pleu
snowing	Il neige.	eel nezh

Do you live here?	*Vous habitez ici?*	voo za·bee·tey ee·see
Where are you going?	*Où allez-vous?*	oo a·ley·voo
What are you doing?	*Que faites-vous?*	ke fet·voo

invitations

Would you like to go (for a) …?	*Tu voudrais aller …?*	tew voo·drey a·ley …
dancing	*danser*	don·sey
drink	*prendre un verre*	pron·dre un vair
meal	*manger*	mon·zhey
out	*sortir*	sor·teer

Yes, I'd love to.
Je viendrai avec plaisir.   zhe vyun·drey a·vek pley·zeer
No, I'm afraid I can't.
Non, désolé, je ne peux pas.   non dey·zo·ley zhe ne peu pa

I love it here!
Ça me plaît beaucoup ici!
sa me pley bo·koo ee·see

What time shall we meet?
On se retrouve à quelle heure?   on se re·troov a kel er
Where will we meet?
On se retrouve où?   on se re·troov oo

Let's meet at …	*On peut se retrouver …*	on peu se rer·troo·vey …
(eight o'clock)	*à (huit heures)*	a (wee ter)
the entrance	*devant l'entrée*	de·von lon·trey

meeting up

Can I …?	*Puis-je …?*	pweezh …
dance with you	*danser avec toi*	don·sey a·vek twa
sit here	*m'asseoir ici*	ma·swar ee·see
take you home	*te raccompagner*	te ra·kom·pa·nyey

37

I'm here with my boyfriend/girlfriend.
Je suis ici avec mon/ma   zhe swee zee·see a·vek mon/ma
petit(e) ami(e). m/f   pe·tee ta·mee

Keep in touch!
Reste en contact!   rest on kon·takt

It's been great meeting you.
Ravi d'avoir fait ta connaissance.   ra·vee da·vwar fey ta ko·ney·sons

likes & dislikes

I thought it was ...	*Je l'ai trouvé ...*	zhe lay troo·vey ...
It's ...	*C'est ...*	sey ...
awful	*horrible*	o·ree·ble
great	*formidable*	for·mee·da·ble
interesting	*intéressant*	un·tey·rey·son

Do you like ...?	*Aimes-tu ...?*	em·tew ...
I like ...	*J'aime ...*	zhem ...
I don't like ...	*Je n'aime pas ...*	zhe nem pa ...
art	*l'art*	lar
shopping	*faire des achets*	fair dey za·sha
sport	*le sport*	le spor

eating & drinking

I'd like ...,	*Je voudrais ...,*	zhe voo·drey ...
please.	*s'il vous plaît.*	seel voo pley
a table for	*une table pour*	ewn ta·ble poor
(five)	*(cinq) personnes*	(sungk) pair·son
the (non)smoking	*un endroit pour*	un on·drwa poor
section	*(non-)fumeurs*	(non·)few·mer

Do you have vegetarian food?
Vous faites les repas végétariens?   voo fet ley re·pa vey·zhey·ta·ryun

What would you recommend?
Qu'est-ce que vous conseillez?   kes·ke voo kon·sey·yey

I'll have a ...	*Je prends ...*	zhe pron ...
Cheers!	*Santé!*	son·tey

French

I'd like (the) …, please.	*Je voudrais …, s'il vous plaît.*	zhe voo·drey … seel voo pley
bill	*l'addition*	la·dee·syon
drink list	*la carte des boissons*	la kart dey bwa·son
menu	*la carte*	la kart
that dish	*ce plat*	ser pla
(cup of) coffee/tea	*(un) café/thé*	(ung) ka·fey/tey
(mineral) water	*eau (minérale)*	o (mee·ney·ral)
bottle of (beer)	*une bouteille de (bière)*	ewn boo·tey de (byair)
glass of (wine)	*un verre de (vin)*	un vair de (vun)
breakfast	*petit déjeuner*	pe·tee dey·zhe·ney
lunch	*déjeuner*	dey·zhe·ney
dinner	*dîner*	dee·ney

Would you like a drink?
Si on buvait quelque chose?
see on bew·vey kel·ke shoz

exploring

Where's the …?	*Où est …?*	oo es …
bank	*la banque*	la bongk
hotel	*l'hôtel*	lo·tel
post office	*le bureau de poste*	le bew·ro de post

Can you show me (on the map)?
Pouvez-vous m'indiquer (sur la carte)?
poo·vey·voo mun·dee·key (sewr la kart)

What time does it open/close?
Quelle est l'heure d'ouverture/ de fermeture?
kel ey leur doo·vair·tewr/ de fer·me·tewr

What's the admission charge?
Quel est le prix d'admission?
kel ey le pree dad·mee·syon

When's the next tour?
C'est quand la prochaine excursion?
sey kon la pro·shen eks·kewr·syon

French

Where can I find ...? *Où sont les ...?* oo son ley ...
   clubs — *clubs* — kleub
   gay venues — *boîtes gaies* — bwat gey
   pubs — *pubs* — peub

Can we get there by public transport?
Peut-on y aller en transport — peu·ton ee a·ley on tran·spor
publique? — pewb·lik

Where can I buy a ticket?
Où peut-on acheter un billet? — oo peu·ton ash·tey um bee·yey

One ... ticket — *Un billet ...* — um bee·yey ...
(to Bordeaux), — *(pour Bordeaux),* — (poor bor·do)
please. — *s'il vous plaît.* — seel voo pley
   one-way — *simple* — sum·ple
   return — *aller et retour* — a·ley ey re·toor

My luggage — *Mes bagages* — mey ba·gazh
has been ... — *ont été ...* — on tey·tey ...
   lost — *perdus* — per·dew
   stolen — *volés* — vo·ley

Is this the ... to — *Est ce ... pour* — es se ... poor
(Nice)? — *(Nice)?* — (nees)
   boat — *le bateau* — le ba·to
   bus — *le bus* — le bews
   plane — *l'avion* — la·vyon
   train — *le train* — le trun

What time's — *Le ... bus passe* — le ... bews pas
the ... bus? — *à quelle heure?* — a kel e
   first — *premier* — pre·myey
   last — *dernier* — dair·nyey
   next — *prochain* — pro·shun

I'd like a taxi ... — *Je voudrais un* — zhe voo·drey un
   taxi ... — tak·see ...
   at (9am) — *à (neuf heures* — a (neu veur
   du matin) — dew ma·tun)
   tomorrow — *demain* — de·mun

How much is it to ...?
C'est combien pour aller à ...? — sey kom·byun poor a·ley a ...

Please take me to (this address).
> *Conduisez-moi à (cette adresse),*
> *s'il vous plaît.*

kon·dwee·zey mwa a (set a·dres)
seel voo pley

Please stop here.
> *Arrêtez-vous ici, s'il vous plaît.*

a·rey·tey voo ee·see seel voo pley

shopping

Where's the (market)?	*Où est (le marché)?*	oo es (le mar·shey)
I'm looking for ...	*Je cherche ...*	zhe shairsh ...
It's faulty.	*C'est défectueux.*	sey dey·fek·tweu
I'd like ..., please.	*Je voudrais ...,* *s'il vous plaît.*	zhe voo·drey ... seel voo pley
a refund	*un remboursement*	un rom·boors·mon
to return this	*rapporter ceci*	ra·por·tey se·see

How much is it?
> *C'est combien?*

sey kom·byun

Can you write down the price?
> *Pouvez-vous écrire le prix?*

poo·vey·voo ey·kreer le pree

That's too expensive.
> *C'est trop cher.*

sey tro shair

There's a mistake in the bill.
> *Il y a une erreur dans la note.*

eel ya ewn ey·reur don la not

I need a film for this camera.
> *J'ai besoin d'une pellicule*
> *pour cet appareil.*

zhey be·zwun dewn pey·lee·kewl
poor sey·ta·pa·rey

Do you accept ...?	*Est-ce que je peux* *payer avec ...?*	es·ke zhe pe pey·yey a·vek ...
credit cards	*une carte de crédit*	ewn kart de krey·dee
travellers cheques	*des chèques de voyages*	dey shek de vwa·yazh
I'd like ..., please.	*Je voudrais ...,* *s'il vous plaît.*	zhe voo·drey ... seel voo pley
a receipt	*un reçu*	un re·sew
my change	*ma monnaie*	ma mo·ney

41

working

I'm attending a ...	Je participe à ...	zhe par·tee·seep a ...
conference	une conférence	ewn kon·fay·rons
course	un stage	un stazh
meeting	une réunion	ewn ray·ew·nyon
trade fair	une foire	ewn fwar
	commerciale	ko·mair·syal

Where's the (business centre)?
Où est (le centre d'affaires)?   oo es (le son·tre da·fair)

I have an appointment with ...
J'ai rendez-vous avec ...   zhay ron·day·voo a·vek ...

I'm with my colleagues.
Je suis avec mes collègues.   zher swee a·vek may ko·leg

Here's my business card.
Voici ma carte.   vwa·see ma kart

That went very well.
Ça s'est très bien passé.   sa say tray byun pa·say

emergencies

Help!	Au secours!	o skoor
Stop!	Arrêtez!	a·rey·tey
Go away!	Allez-vous-en!	a·ley·voo·zon
Thief!	Au voleur!	o vo·leur
Fire!	Au feu!	o feu

Call ...!	Appelez ...!	a·pley ...
an ambulance	une ambulance	ewn om·bew·lons
a doctor	un médecin	un meyd·sun
the police	la police	la po·lees

Could you help me, please?	Est-ce que vous pourriez m'aider, s'il vous plaît?	es·ke voo poo·ryey mey·dey seel voo pley
I'm lost.	Je suis perdu(e). m/f	zhe swee pair·dew
Where are the toilets?	Où sont les toilettes?	oo son ley twa·let

42

French

German

Germany is the powerhouse of Central Europe, geographically, politically and culturally.

Pronunciation

Vowels		Consonants	
Symbol	**English sound**	**Symbol**	**English sound**
a	run	b	bed
aa	father	ch	cheat
ai	aisle	d	dog
air	fair	f	fat
aw	saw	g	go
e	bet	h	hat
ee	see	k	kit
eu	nurse	kh	loch (guttural)
ew	ee pronounced with rounded lips	l	lot
ey	as in 'bet', but longer	m	man
i	hit	n	not
o	pot	ng	ring
oo	zoo	p	pet
ow	now	r	run (throaty)
oy	toy	s	sun
u	put	sh	shot
		t	top
		ts	hits
		v	very
		y	yes
		z	zero
		zh	pleasure

The German pronunciation is given in blue after each word or phrase. Read these words as though you were reading English and you're sure to be understood. Each syllable is separated by a dot, and italics indicate that you need to put stress on that syllable, for example:

Danke. dang·ke

German

essentials

Yes/No.	*Ja/Nein.*	yaa/nain
Hello.	*Guten Tag.*	goo·ten taak
Goodbye.	*Auf Wiedersehen.*	owf vee·der·zey·en
Please.	*Bitte.*	bi·te
Thank you.	*Danke.*	dang·ke
Thank you very much.	*Vielen Dank.*	fee·len dangk
You're welcome.	*Bitte.*	bi·te
Excuse me/Sorry.	*Entschuldigung.*	ent·shul·di·gung

Do you speak English?
Sprechen Sie Englisch?   shpre·khen zee eng·lish

Do you understand?
Verstehen Sie?   fer·shtey·en zee

I (don't) understand.
Ich verstehe (nicht).   ikh fer·shtey·e (nikht)

chatting

introductions

| Mr | *Herr* | her |
| Mrs/Miss | *Frau/Fräulein* | frow/froy·lain |

How are you?	*Wie geht es Ihnen?*	vee geyt es ee·nen
Fine.	*Danke, gut.*	dang·ke goot
And you?	*Und Ihnen?*	unt ee·nen
What's your name?	*Wie ist Ihr Name?*	vee ist eer naa·me
My name is ...	*Mein Name ist ...*	main naa·me ist ...
I'm pleased to meet you.	*Angenehm.*	an·ge·neym

Here's my ...	*Hier ist meine ...*	heer ist mai·ne ...
What's your...?	*Wie ist Ihre ...?*	vee ist ee·re ...
(email) address	*(E-mail-)Adresse*	(ee·mayl·)a·dre·se
phone number	*Telefonnummer*	te·le·fawn·nu·mer

45

What's your occupation?

Als was arbeiten Sie? pol		als vas *ar*·bai·ten zee
Als was arbeitest du? inf		als vas *ar*·bai·test doo

I'm a ...	*Ich bin ein/*	ikh bin ain/
	eine ... m/f	*ai*·ne ...
businessperson	*Geschäftsmann* m	ge·*shefts*·man
	Geschäftsfrau f	ge·*shefts*·frow
student	*Student* m	shtu·*dent*
	Studentin f	shtu·*den*·tin

Where are you from?

Woher kommen Sie? pol		vaw·hair *ko*·men zee
Woher kommst du? inf		vaw·hair komst doo

I'm from (England).

Ich komme aus (England).	ikh *ko*·me ows (*eng*·lant)

Are you married?

Sind Sie verheiratet? pol		zint zee fer·*hai*·ra·tet
Bist du verheiratet? inf		bist doo fer·*hai*·ra·tet

I'm married/single.

Ich bin verheiratet/ledig.	ikh bin fer·*hai*·ra·tet/*ley*·dikh

How old are you?

Wie alt sind Sie? pol		vee alt zint zee
Wie alt bist du? inf		vee alt bist doo

I'm ... years old.

Ich bin ... Jahre alt.	ikh bin ... *yaa*·re alt

making conversation

What's the weather like?

Wie ist das Wetter?	vee ist das *ve*·ter

It's ...		
cold	*Es ist kalt.*	es ist kalt
hot	*Es ist heiß.*	es ist hais
raining	*Es regnet.*	es *reyg*·net
snowing	*Es schneit.*	es shnait

Do you live here?

Wohnen Sie hier?	*vaw*·nen zee heer

Where are you going?
Wohin fahren Sie? vaw·hin faa·ren zee

What are you doing?
Was machen Sie? vas ma·khen zee

invitations

Would you like	Möchten Sie	meukh·ten zee
to go (for a) …?	… gehen?	… gey·en
dancing	tanzen	tan·tsen
drink	etwas trinken	et·vas tring·ken
meal	essen	e·sen
out	aus	ows

Yes, I'd love to.
Ja, gerne. yaa ger·ne

No, I'm afraid I can't.
Nein, es tut mir Leid, nain es toot meer lait
aber ich kann nicht. aa·ber ikh kan nikht

I love it here!
Mir gefällt es hier sehr gut!
meer ge·*felt* es heer zair goot

Where/When shall we meet?
Wo/Wann sollen wir uns treffen? vaw/van zo·len veer uns tre·fen

Let's meet at …	Wir treffen uns …	veer tre·fen uns …
(eight) o'clock	um (acht) Uhr	um (akht) oor
the entrance	am Eingang	am ain·gang

meeting up

Can I …?	Darf ich …?	darf ikh …
dance with you	mit dir tanzen	mit deer tan·tsen
sit here	hier sitzen	heer zi·tsen
take you home	dich nach Hause	dikh nahkh how·ze
	bringen	bring·en

German

I'm here with ...	Ich bin mit ... hier.	ikh bin mit ... heer
my boyfriend	meinem Freund	mai·nem froynt
my girlfriend	meiner Freundin	mai·ner froyn·din

Keep in touch!
Melde dich mal! — mel·de dikh maal

It's been great meeting you.
Es war schön, dich — es vaar sheun dikh
kennen zu lernen. — ke·nen tsoo ler·nen

likes & dislikes

It is/was ...	Es ist/war ...	es ist/vahr ...
awful	schrecklich	shrek·likh
great	toll	tol
interesting	interessant	in·tre·sant

Do you like ...?	Magst du ...?	maakst doo ...
I (don't) like ...	Ich mag (keine/	ikh maak (kai·ne/
	keinen) ... m/f	kai·nen) ...
art	Kunst f	kunst
sport	Sport m	shport

I (don't) like shopping.
Ich kaufe (nicht) gern ein. — ikh kow·fe (nikht) gern ain

And you?
Und du? — unt doo

eating & drinking

I'd like ...,	Ich hätte gern	ikh he·te gern
please.	..., bitte.	... bi·te
a table for (five)	einen Tisch für	ai·nen tish fewr
	(fünf) Personen	(fewnf) per·zaw·nen
the (non)smoking	einen (Nicht-)	ai·nen (nikht·)
section	rauchertisch	row·kher·tish

Do you have vegetarian food?
Haben Sie vegetarisches Essen? — haa·ben zee ve·ge·taa·ri·shes e·sen

What would you recommend?
Was empfehlen Sie? — vas emp·fey·len zee

| I'll have ... | Ich hätte gern ... | ikh *he*·te gern ... |
| Cheers! | Prost! | prawst |

I'd like (the) ..., please.	Bitte bringen Sie ...	*bi*·te *bring*·en zee ...
bill	die Rechnung	dee *rekh*·nung
drink list	die Getränkekarte	dee ge·*treng*·ke·kar·te
menu	die Speisekarte	dee *shpai*·ze·kar·te
that dish	dieses Gericht	*dee*·zes ge·*rikht*

(cup of) coffee/tea	(eine Tasse) Kaffee/Tee	(*ai*·ne *ta*·se) *ka*·fey/tey
mineral water	Mineralwasser	mi·ne·*raal*·va·ser
bottle of (beer)	eine Flasche (Bier)	*ai*·ne *fla*·she (beer)
glass of (wine)	ein Glas (Wein)	ain glaas (vain)

Would you like a drink?
Möchtest du etwas trinken?
meukh·test doo *et*·vas *tring*·ken

German

breakfast	Frühstück	*frew*·shtewk
lunch	Mittagessen	*mi*·taak·e·sen
dinner	Abendessen	*aa*·bent·e·sen

exploring

Where's the ...?	Wo ist ...?	vaw ist ...
bank	die Bank	dee bangk
hotel	das Hotel	das ho·*tel*
post office	das Postamt	das *post*·amt

Can you show me (on the map)?
Können Sie es mir *keu*·nen zee es meer
(auf der Karte) zeigen? (owf dair *kar*·te) *tsai*·gen

What time does it open/close?
Wann macht es auf/zu? van makht es owf/tsoo

What's the admission charge?
Was kostet der Eintritt? vas *kos*·tet dair *ain*·trit

When's the next tour?
Wann ist die nächste Tour? van ist dee *neykhs*·te toor

Where can I find ...?	Wo sind die ...?	vaw zint dee ...
clubs	Klubs	klups
gay venues	Schwulenkneipen	shvoo·len·knai·pen
pubs	Kneipen	knai·pen

Can we get there by public transport?

Gelangen wir mit öffentlichen Verkehrsmitteln dort hin?	ge·lang·en veer mit eu·fent·li·khen fer·kers·mi·teln dort hin

Where can I buy a ticket?

Wo kann ich eine Fahrkarte kaufen?	vaw kan ikh ai·ne faar·kar·te kow·fen

One ...ticket to (Berlin), please.	Einen ... nach (Berlin), bitte.	ai·nen ... naakh (ber·leen) bi·te
one-way	einfache Fahrkarte	ain·fa·khe faar·kar·te
return	Rückfahrkarte	rewk·faar·kar·te

My luggage has been ...	Mein Gepäck ist ...	main ge·pek ist ...
lost	verloren gegangen	fer·law·ren ge·gang·en
stolen	gestohlen worden	ge·shtaw·len vor·den

Is this the ... to (Hamburg)?	Fährt ... nach (Hamburg)?	fairt ... nakh (ham·burg)
boat	das Boot	das bawt
bus	der Bus	dair bus
plane	das Flugzeug	das flook·tsoyk
train	der Zug	dair tsook

What time's the ... bus?	Wann fährt der ... Bus?	van fairt dair ... bus
first	erste	ers·te
last	letzte	lets·te
next	nächste	neykhs·te

I'd like a taxi ...	Ich hätte gern ein Taxi für ...	ikh he·te gern ain tak·si fewr ...
at (9am)	(neun Uhr vormittags)	(noyn oor fawr·mi·taaks)
tomorrow	morgen	mor·gen

How much is it to ...?
Was kostet es bis ...?   vas *kos*·tet es bis ...

Please take me to (this address).
Bitte bringen Sie mich zu   *bi*·te *bring*·en zee mikh tsoo
(dieser Adresse).   (*dee*·zer a·*dre*·se)

Please stop here.
Bitte halten Sie hier.   *bi*·te *hal*·ten zee heer

shopping

Where's (the market)?	*Wo ist (der Markt)?*	vaw ist (dair markt)
I'm looking for ...	*Ich suche nach ...*	ikh *zoo*·khe nakh ...
It's faulty.	*Es ist fehlerhaft.*	es ist *fey*·ler·haft
I'd like ..., please.	*Ich möchte bitte ...*	ikh *meukh*·te *bi*·te ...
a refund	*mein Geld*	main gelt
	zurückhaben	tsu·*rewk*·haa·ben
to return this	*dieses zurück-*	*dee*·zes tsu·*rewk*·
	geben	*gey*·ben
How much is it?	*Wie viel kostet das?*	vee feel *kos*·tet das
That's too expensive.	*Das ist zu teuer.*	das ist tsoo *toy*·er

Can you write down the price?
Können Sie den Preis   *keu*·nen zee deyn prais
aufschreiben?   *owf*·shrai·ben

There's a mistake in the bill.
Da ist ein Fehler in der Rechnung.   daa ist ain *fey*·ler in dair *rekh*·nung

I need a film for this camera.
Ich brauche einen   ikh *brow*·khe *ai*·nen
Film für diese Kamera.   film fewr *dee*·ze *ka*·me·ra

Do you accept ...?	*Nehmen Sie ...?*	*ney*·men zee ...
credit cards	*Kreditkarten*	kre·*deet*·kar·ten
travellers cheques	*Reiseschecks*	*rai*·ze·sheks
I'd like ..., please.	*Ich möchte bitte ...*	ikh *meukh*·te *bi*·te ...
a receipt	*eine Quittung*	*ai*·ne *kvi*·tung
my change	*mein Wechselgeld*	main *vek*·sel·gelt

51

working

I'm attending a ...	*Ich nehme an ... teil.*	ikh *ney*·me an ... tail
conference	*einer Konferenz*	*ai*·ner kon·fe·*rents*
course	*einem Kurs*	*ai*·nem kurs
meeting	*einem Meeting*	*ai*·nem *mee*·ting

Where's the (business centre)?
Wo ist (das Tagungszentrum)?   vaw ist (das *taa*·gungks·tsen·trum)

I'm visiting a trade fair.
Ich besuche eine Messe.   ikh be·*zoo*·khe *ai*·ne *me*·se

I have an appointment with ...
Ich habe einen Termin bei ...   ikh *haa*·be *ai*·nen ter·*meen* bai ...

I'm with my colleagues.
Ich bin mit meinen Kollegen/   ikh bin mit *mai*·nen ko·*ley*·gen/
Kolleginnen hier. m/f   ko·*ley*·gi·nen heer

Here's my business card.
Hier ist meine Karte.   heer ist *mai*·ne *kar*·te

That went very well.
Das war sehr gut.   das vaar zair goot

emergencies

Help!	*Hilfe!*	*hil*·fe
Stop!	*Halt!*	halt
Go away!	*Gehen Sie weg!*	*gey*·en zee vek
Thief!	*Dieb!*	deeb
Fire!	*Feuer!*	*foy*·er

Call ...!	*Rufen Sie ...!*	*roo*·fen zee ...
an ambulance	*einen Kranken-*	*ai*·nen *krang*·ken·
	wagen	vaa·gen
a doctor	*einen Arzt*	*ai*·nen artst
the police	*die Polizei*	dee po·li·*tsai*

Could you help me, please?	*Könnten Sie mir bitte helfen?*	*keun*·ten zee meer *bi*·te *hel*·fen
I'm lost.	*Ich habe mich verirrt.*	ikh *haa*·be mikh fer·*irt*
Where are the toilets?	*Wo ist die Toilette?*	vo ist dee to·a·*le*·te

Greek

You cannot wander far in Greece without stumbling across Europe's greatest ages — whether it be a broken column or a tiny Byzantine church — all snapshots of former glory.

Pronunciation

Vowels		Consonants	
Symbol	English sound	Symbol	English sound
a	f**a**ther	b	**b**ed
e	b**e**t	d	**d**og
i	h**i**t	dh	**th**at
ia	nostalg**ia**	dz	a**dds**
io	rat**io**	f	**f**at
o	p**o**t	g	**g**o
u	p**u**t	gh	guttural sound, between 'goat' and 'loch'

The Greek pronunciation is given in blue after each word or phrase. Read these words as though you were reading English and you're sure to be understood. Each syllable is separated by a dot, and italics indicate that you need to put stress on that syllable, for example:

Παρακαλώ.   pa·ra·ka·*lo*

h	**h**at
k	**k**it
kh	lo**ch** (guttural sound)
l	**l**et
m	**m**an
n	**n**ot
ng	ri**ng**
p	**p**et
r	**r**ed (trilled)
s	**s**un
t	**t**op
th	**th**in
ts	ha**ts**
v	**v**ery
y	**y**es
z	**z**ero

essentials

Yes/No.	Ναι/Όχι.	ne/o·hi
Hello/Goodbye.	Γεια σου/Αντίο.	yia su/a·di·o
Please.	Παρακαλώ.	pa·ra·ka·lo
Thank you	Ευχαριστώ	ef·kha·ri·sto
(very much).	(πολύ).	(po·li)
You're welcome.	Παρακαλώ.	pa·ra·ka·lo
Excuse me.	Με συγχωρείτε.	me sing·kho·ri·te
Sorry.	Συγνώμη.	si·ghno·mi

Do you speak English?
Μιλάς Αγγλικά;   mi·las ang·gli·ka

Do you understand?
Καταλαβαίνεις;   ka·ta·la·ve·nis

I (don't) understand.
(Δεν) Καταλαβαίνω.   (dhen) ka·ta·la·ve·no

chatting

introductions

Mr	Κύριε	ki·ri·e
Mrs/Miss	Κυρία/Δις	ki·ri·a/dhes·pi·nis
How are you?	Τι κάνεις;	ti ka·nis
Fine. And you?	Καλά. Εσύ;	ka·la e·si
What's your name?	Πως σε λένε;	pos se le·ne
My name is ...	Με λένε ...	me le·ne ...
I'm pleased to meet you.	Χαίρω πολύ.	he·ro po·li

Here's my address.
Εδώ είναι η διεύθυνσή μου.   e·dho i·ne i dhi·ef·thin·si mu

What's your address?
Ποια είναι η δική σου διεύθυνση;   pia i·ne i dhi·ki su dhi·ef·thin·si

Here's my ...	Εδώ είναι ... μου.	e·dho i·ne ... mu
What's your ...?	Ποιο είναι ... σου;	pio i·ne ... su
email address	το ημέιλ	to i·me·il
phone number	το τηλέφωνό	to ti·le·fo·no

What's your occupation?

Τι δουλειά κάνεις;   ti dhu·lia ka·nis

I'm a ...	Είμαι ...	i·me ...
businessperson	επιχειρηματίας	e·pi·hi·ri·ma·ti·as
student	σπουδαστής m	spu·dha·stis
	σπουδάστρια f	spu·dha·stri·a

Where are you from?

Από που είσαι;   a·po pu i·se

I'm from (England).

Είμαι από την (Αγγλία).   i·me a·po tin (ang·gli·a)

Are you married?	Είσαι παντρεμένος/	i·se pa·dre·me·nos/
	παντρεμένη; m/f	pa·dre·me·ni
I'm married.	Είμαι παντρεμένος/	i·me pa·dre·me·nos/
	παντρεμένη. m/f	pa·dre·me·ni
I'm single.	Είμαι ανύπαντρος/	i·me a·ni·pa·dros/
	ανύπαντρη. m/f	a·ni·pa·dri
How old are you?	Πόσο χρονών είσαι;	po·so khro·non i·se
I'm ... years old.	Είμαι ... χρονών.	i·me ... khro·non

making conversation

What's the weather like?

Πως είναι ο καιρός;   pos i·ne o ke·ros

It's ...		
cold	Κάνει κρύο.	ka·ni kri·o
hot	Κάνει πολλή ζέστη.	ka·ni po·li ze·sti
raining	Βρέχει.	vre·hi
snowing	Χιονίζει.	hio·ni·zi

Do you live here?	Μένεις εδώ;	me·nis e·dho
Where are you going?	Πού πηγαίνεις;	pu pi·ye·nis
What are you doing?	Τι κάνεις;	ti ka·nis

56

invitations

Would you like to go (for a) ...?	Θα ήθελες να πας ...;	tha *i*-the-les na pas ...
dancing	για χορό	yia kho-*ro*
drink	για ποτό	yia po-*to*
meal	για φαγητό	yia fa-yi-*to*
out	κάπου έξω	*ka*-pu *ek*-so

Yes, I'd love to.
Ναι, θα ήθελα πολύ. ne tha *i*-the-la po-*li*

No, I'm afraid I can't.
Όχι, φοβάμαι πως δεν μπορώ. *o*-hi fo-*va*-me pos dhen bo-*ro*

I love it here!
Μου αρέσει εδώ!
mu a-*re*-si e-*dho*

What time will we meet?
Τι ώρα θα συναντηθούμε; ti *o*-ra tha si-na-di-*thu*-me

Where will we meet?
Πού θα συναντηθούμε; pu tha si-na-di-*thu*-me

Let's meet at ...	Ας συναντηθούμε ...	as si-na-di-*thu*-me ...
(eight) o'clock	στις (οχτώ)	stis (okh-*to*)
the entrance	στην είσοδο	stin *i*-so-dho

meeting up

Can I ...?	Μπορώ να ...;	bo-*ro* na ...
dance with you	χορέψω μαζί σου	kho-*rep*-so ma-*zi* su
sit here	καθίσω εδώ	ka-*thi*-so e-*dho*
take you home	σε πάρω στο σπίτι	se *pa*-ro sto *spi*-ti

I'm here with my boyfriend.
Είμαι εδώ με τον φίλο μου. *i*-me e-*dho* me ton *fi*-lo mu

I'm here with my girlfriend.
Είμαι εδώ με την φίλη μου. *i*-me e-*dho* me tin *fi*-li mu

Keep in touch!

Μη χαθούμε! — mi kha·*thu*·me

It's been great meeting you.

Είναι υπέροχο που σε — *i*·ne i·*pe*·ro·kho pu se
συνάντησα. — si·*na*·di·sa

likes & dislikes

I thought it was ...	Νομίζω ήταν ...	no·*mi*·zo *i*·tan ...
It's ...	Είναι ...	*i*·ne ...
awful	απαίσιο	a·*pe*·si·o
great	καταπληκτικό	ka·ta·plik·ti·*ko*
interesting	ενδιαφέρον	en·dhia·*fe*·ron
Do you like ...?	Σου αρέσουν ...;	su a·*re*·sun ...
I (don't) like ...	(Δεν) Μου αρέσουν	(dhen) mu a·*re*·sun
	τα ...	ta ...
art	καλλιτεχνικά	ka·li·*tekh*·ni·*ka*
sport	σπορ	spor

Do you like shopping?

Σου αρέσει να ψωνίζεις; — su a·*re*·si na pso·*ni*·zis

I (don't) like shopping.

(Δεν) Μου αρέσει να ψωνίζω. — (dhen) mu a·*re*·si na pso·*ni*·zo

eating & drinking

I'd like ..., please.	Θα ήθελα ...,	tha *i*·thela ...
	παρακαλώ.	pa·ra·ka·*lo*
a table for (five)	ένα τραπέζι για	*e*·na tra·*pe*·zi yia
	(πέντε)	(*pe*·de)
the (non)smoking	στους (μη)	stus (mi)
section	καπνίζοντες	kap·*ni*·zo·des

Do you have vegetarian food?

Εχετε φαγητό για χορτοφάγους; — *e*·he·te fa·yi·*to* yia khor·to·*fa*·ghus

What would you recommend?

Τι θα συνιστούσες; — ti tha si·ni·*stu*·ses

| I'll have a ... | Θα πάρω ... | tha *pa*·ro ... |
| Cheers! | Εις υγείαν! | is i·*yi*·an |

I'd like (a/the) ...,	Θα ήθελα ...,	tha *i*·the·la ...
please.	παρακαλώ.	pa·ra·ka·*lo*
bill	το λογαριασμό	to lo·gha·riaz·*mo*
drink list	τον κατάλογο	ton ka·*ta*·lo·gho
	με τα ποτά	me ta po·*ta*
menu	το μενού	to me·*nu*
that dish	εκείνο το φαγητό	e·*ki*·no to fa·yi·*to*

Would you like a drink?
Θα ήθελες ένα ποτό;
tha *i*·the·les *e*·na po·*to*

coffee/tea	καφέ/τσάι	ka·*fe*/*tsa*·i
(mineral) water	(μεταλλικό) νερό	(me·ta·li·*ko*) ne·*ro*
bottle of (beer)	ένα μπουκάλι (μπύρα)	*e*·na bu·*ka*·li (*bi*·ra)
glass of (wine)	ένα ποτήρι (κρασί)	*e*·na po·*ti*·ri (kra·*si*)

breakfast	πρόγευμα	*pro*·yev·ma
lunch	γεύμα	*yev*·ma
dinner	δείπνο	*dhip*·no

exploring

Where's the ...?	Που είναι ...?	pu *i*·ne ...
bank	η τράπεζα	i *tra*·pe·za
hotel	το ξενοδοχείο	to kse·no·dho·*hi*·o
post office	το ταχυδρομείο	to ta·hi·dhro·*mi*·o

Can you show me (on the map)?

| Μπορείς να μου δείξεις | bo·*ris* na mu *dhik*·sis |
| (στο χάρτη); | (sto *khar*·ti) |

What time does it open/close?

| Τι ώρα ανοίγει/κλείνει; | ti *o*·ra a·*ni*·yi/*kli*·ni |

59

What's the admission charge?

Πόσο κοστίζει η είσοδος;   *po*·so ko·*sti*·zi i *i*·so·dhos

When's the next tour?

Πότε είναι η επόμενη περιήγηση;   *po*·te *i*·ne i e·*po*·me·ni pe·ri·*i*·yi·si

Where can I find ...?	Που μπορώ να βρω ...;	pu bo·*ro* na vro ...
clubs	κλαμπ	klab
gay venues	Χώρους συνάντησης για γκέη	*kho*·rus si·*na*·di·sis yia *ge*·i
pubs	μπυραρίες	bi·ra·*ri*·es

Can we get there by public transport?

Μπορούμε να το φτάσουμε με τις δημόσιες συγκοινωνίες;   bo·*ru*·me na to *fta*·su·me me tis dhi·*mo*·si·es sin·gi·no·*ni*·es

Where can I buy a ticket?

Που αγοράζω εισιτήριο;   pu a·gho·*ra*·zo i·si·*ti*·ri·o

My luggage has been lost/stolen.

Οι αποσκευές μου έχουν χαθεί/κλαπεί.   i a·pos·ke·*ves* mu *e*·khun kha·*thi*/kla·*pi*

One ... ticket to (Patras), please.	Ένα εισιτήριο ... για την (Πάτρα), παρακαλώ.	*e*·na i·si·*ti*·ri·o ... yia tin (*pa*·tra) pa·ra·ka·*lo*
one-way	απλό	a·*plo*
return	με επιστροφή	me e·pi·stro·*fi*

Is this the ... to (Athens)?	Είναι αυτό το ... για την (Αθήνα);	*i*·ne af·*to* to ... yia tin (a·*thi*·na)
boat	πλοίο	*pli*·o
bus	λεωφορείο	le·o·fo·*ri*·o
plane	αεροπλάνο	a·e·ro·*pla*·no
train	τρένο	*tre*·no

What time's the ... (bus)?	Πότε είναι το ... (λεωφορείο);	*po*·te *i*·ne to ... (le·o·fo·*ri*·o)
first	πρώτο	*pro*·to
last	τελευταίο	te·lef·*te*·o
next	επόμενο	e·*po*·me·no

I'd like a taxi ...	Θα ήθελα ένα ταξί ...	tha *i*·the·la *e*·na tak·*si* ...
at (9am)	στις (εννέα) πριν το μεσημέρι	stis (e·*ne*·a ... prin to me·si·*me*·ri)
tomorrow	αύριο	*av*·ri·o

60

Greek

How much is it to …?
Πόσο κάνει για …; po·so ka·ni yia …

Please take me to (this address).
Παρακαλώ πάρε με σε pa·ra·ka·lo pa·re me se
(αυτή τη διεύθυνση). (af·ti ti dhi·ef·thin·si)

Please stop here.
Παρακαλώ σταμάτα εδώ. pa·ra·ka·lo sta·ma·ta e·dho

shopping

Where's the (market)?	Που είναι (η αγορά)?	pu i·ne (i a·gho·ra)
I'd like to buy …	Θα ήθελα να αγοράσω …	tha i·the·la na a·gho·ra·so …
It's faulty.	Είναι ελαττωματικό.	i·ne e·la·to·ma·ti·ko
I'd like …, please.	Θα ήθελα …, παρακαλώ.	tha i·the·la … pa·ra·ka·lo
my change	τα ρέστα μου	ta re·sta mu
a refund	επιστροφή χρημάτων	e·pi·stro·fi khri·ma·ton
to return this	να επιστρέψω αυτό	na e·pi·strep·so af·to

How much is it?
Πόσο κάνει; po·so ka·ni

Can you write down the price?
Μπορείς να γράψεις την τιμή; bo·ris na ghrap·sis tin ti·mi

That's too expensive.
Είναι πάρα πολύ ακριβό. i·ne pa·ra po·li a·kri·vo

There's a mistake in the bill.
Υπάρχει κάποιο λάθος i·par·hi ka·pio la·thos
στο λογαριασμό. sto lo·gha·riaz·mo

Can I have a receipt, please?
Μπορώ να έχω μια bo·ro na e·kho mia
απόδειξη, παρακαλώ; a·po·dhik·si pa·ra·ka·lo

Do you accept …?	Δέχεστε …;	dhe·he·ste …
credit cards	πιστωτικές κάρτες	pi·sto·ti·kes kar·tes
travellers	ταξιδιωτικές	tak·si·dhio·ti·kes
cheques	επιταγές	e·pi·ta·yes

working

Where's the (business centre)?
Πού είναι (ο χώρος εργασίας);   pu *i*·ne (o *kho*·ros er·gha·*si*·as)

I'm attending a ...   Παρακολουθώ ...   pa·ra·ko·lu·*tho* ...
conference   ένα συνέδριο   *e*·na sin·*e*·dhri·o
course   μια σειρά   mia si·*ra*
     μαθημάτων   ma·thi·*ma*·ton
meeting   μια συνεδρίαση   mia sin·e·*dhri*·a·si
trade fair   μια εμπορική   mia e·bo·ri·*ki*
     έκθεση   *ek*·the·si

I have an appointment with ...
Έχω ένα ραντεβού με ...   *e*·kho *e*·na ra·de·*vu* me ...
I'm with my colleagues.
Είμαι με τους συναδέλφους μου.   *i*·me me tus sin·a·*dhel*·fus mu
Here's my business card.
Ορίστε η κάρτα μου.   o·*ri*·ste i *kar*·ta mu
That went very well.
Πήγε πολύ καλά.   *pi*·ye po·*li* ka·*la*

emergencies

Help!   Βοήθεια!   vo·*i*·thia
Stop!   Σταμάτα!   sta·*ma*·ta
Go away!   Φύγε!   *fi*·ye
Thief!   Κλέφτης!   *klef*·tis
Fire!   Φωτιά!   fo·*tia*

Call ...!   Κάλεσε ...!   ka·le·se ...
an ambulance   το ασθενοφόρο   to as·the·no·*fo*·ro
the doctor   ένα γιατρό   *e*·na yia·*tro*
the police   την αστυνομία   tin a·sti·no·*mi*·a

Could you help me,   Μπορείς να βοηθήσεις,   bo·*ris* na vo·i·*thi*·sis
please?   παρακαλώ;   pa·ra·ka·*lo*
I'm lost.   Έχω χαθεί.   *e*·kho kha·*thi*
Where are the   Πού είναι η   pu *i*·ne i
toilets?   τουαλέτα;   tu·a·*le*·ta

Italian

"
Rare is the traveller who isn't smitten by Italy.
"

Pronunciation

Vowels		Consonants	
Symbol	English sound	Symbol	English sound
a	father	b	bed
ai	aisle	ch	cheat
ay	say	d	dog
e	bet	dz	adds
ee	see	f	fat
o	pot	g	go
oo	zoo	j	joke
oy	toy	k	kit
ow	how	l	lot
		ly	million
		m	man
		n	not
		ny	canyon
		p	pet
		r	red (stronger and rolled)
		s	sun
		sh	shot
		t	top
		ts	hits
		v	very
		w	win
		y	yes
		z	zero

The Italian pronunciation is given in blue after each word or phrase. Read these words as though you were reading English and you're sure to be understood. Each syllable is separated by a dot, and italics indicate that you need to put stress on that syllable, for example:

Buongiorno.   bwon·*jor*·no

essentials

Yes/No.	*Sì/No.*	see/no
Hello.	*Buongiorno.*	bwon·*jor*·no
Goodbye.	*Arrivederci.*	a·ree·ve·*der*·chee
Please.	*Per favore.*	per fa·*vo*·re
Thank you (very much).	*Grazie (mille).*	*gra*·tsye (*mee*·le)
You're welcome.	*Prego.*	*pre*·go
Excuse me.	*Mi scusi.* pol	mee *skoo*·zee
	Scusami. inf	*skoo*·za·mee
Sorry.	*Mi dispiace.*	mee dees·*pya*·che
Do you speak English?	*Parla inglese?*	*par*·la een·*gle*·ze
Do you understand?	*Capisce?*	ka·*pee*·she
I (don't) understand.	*(Non) Capisco.*	(non) ka·*pee*·sko

chatting

introductions

Mr	*Signore*	see·*nyo*·re
Mrs/Miss	*Signora/Signorina*	see·*nyo*·ra/see·nyo·*ree*·na
How are you?	*Come sta/stai?* pol/inf	*ko*·me sta/stai
Fine. And you?	*Bene. E Lei/tu?* pol/inf	*be*·ne e lay/too
What's your name?	*Come si chiama?* pol	*ko*·me see *kya*·ma
	Come ti chiami? inf	*ko*·me tee *kya*·mee
My name is ...	*Mi chiamo ...*	mee *kya*·mo ...
I'm pleased to meet you.	*Piacere.*	pya·*che*·re
Here's my ...	*Ecco il mio ...*	*e*·ko eel *mee*·o ...
What's your ...?	*Qual'è il*	kwa·*le* eel
	Suo/tuo ...? pol/inf	*soo*·o/*too*·o ...
(email) address	*indirizzo (di email)*	een·dee·*ree*·tso (dee e·mayl)
phone number	*numero di telefono*	*noo*·me·ro dee te·*le*·fo·no

65

Italian

Italian

What's your occupation?
Che lavoro fa/fai? pol/inf   ke la·*vo*·ro fa/fai

I'm a ...   *Sono ...*   *so*·no ...
  businessperson   *uomo/donna*   *wo*·mo/*do*·na
                        d'affari m/f   da·*fa*·ree
  student   *studente* m   stoo·*den*·te
                        studentessa f   stoo·den·*te*·sa

Where are you from?
Da dove viene/vieni? pol/inf   da *do*·ve *vye*·ne/*vye*·nee

I'm from (England).
Vengo (dall'Inghilterra).   *ven*·go (da·leen·geel·*te*·ra)

Are you married?
È sposato/sposata? m/f pol   e spo·*za*·to/spo·*za*·ta
Sei sposato/sposata? m/f inf   say spo·*za*·to/spo·*za*·ta

I'm married.
Sono sposato/sposata. m/f   *so*·no spo·*za*·to/spo·*za*·ta

I'm single.
Sono celibe/nubile. m/f   *so*·no *che*·lee·be/*noo*·bee·le

How old are you?
Quanti anni ha/hai? pol/inf   *kwan*·tee *a*·nee a/ai

I'm ... years old.
Ho ... anni.   o ... *a*·nee

making conversation

What's the weather like?
Che tempo fa?   ke *tem*·po fa

It's ...
  cold   *Fa freddo.*   fa *fre*·do
  hot   *Fa caldo.*   fa *kal*·do
  raining   *Piove.*   *pyo*·ve
  snowing   *Nevica.*   ne·*vee*·ka

Do you live here?   *Lei è di qui?* pol   lay e dee kwee
                  Tu sei di qui? inf   too say dee kwee
Where are you going?   *Dove va/vai?* pol/inf   *do*·ve va/vai
What are you doing?   *Che fa/fai?* pol/inf   ke fa/fai

invitations

Would you like to go (for a) …?	Volete/Vuoi andare a …? pol/inf	vo·le·te/vwoy an·da·re a …
dancing	ballare	ba·la·re
drink	bere qualcosa	be·re kwal·ko·za
meal	mangiare qualcosa	man·ja·re kwal·ko·za
out	spasso	spa·so

Yes, I'd love to.
Sì, mi piacerebbe molto. see mee pya·che·re·be mol·to

No, I'm afraid I can't.
No, temo di no. no te·mo dee no

I love it here!
Mi piace molto qua!
mee *pya*·che *mol*·to kwa

What time shall we meet?
A che ora ci vediamo? a ke o·ra chee ve·dya·mo

Where will we meet?
Dove ci vediamo? do·ve chee ve·dya·mo

Let's meet at …	Incontriamoci …	een·kon·trya·mo·chee …
(eight) o'clock	alle (otto)	a·le (o·to)
the entrance	all'entrata	a·len·tra·ta

meeting up

Can I …?	Posso …?	po·so …
dance with you	ballare con te	ba·la·re kon te
sit here	sedermi qui	se·der·mee kwee
take you home	accompagnarti a casa	a·kom·pa·nyar·tee a ka·za

I'm here with my boyfriend.
Sono qui con il mio ragazzo. so·no kwee kon eel mee·o ra·ga·tso

I'm here with my girlfriend.
Sono qui con la mia ragazza. so·no kwee kon la mee·a ra·ga·tsa

Italian

Keep in touch!
   Teniamoci in contatto!   te·*nya*·mo·chee een kon·*ta*·to

It's been great meeting you.
   È stato veramente un   e *sta*·to ve·ra·*men*·te oon
   piacere conoscerti.   pya·*che*·re ko·no·*sher*·tee

likes & dislikes

I thought it was ...	*Lo/La trovavo ...* m/f	lo/la tro·*va*·vo ...
It's ...	*È ...*	e ...
awful	*schifoso* m	skee·*fo*·so
	schifosa f	skee·*fo*·sa
great	*meraviglioso* m	me·ra·vee·*lyo*·so
	meravigliosa f	me·ra·vee·*lyo*·sa
interesting	*interessante* m&f	een·te·re·*san*·te
Do you like ...?	*Ti piace ...?*	tee *pya*·che ...
I (don't) like ...	*(Non) Mi piace ...*	(non) mee *pya*·che ...
art	*l'arte*	*lar*·te
shopping	*lo shopping*	lo *sho*·ping
sport	*lo sport*	lo sport

eating & drinking

I'd like ...,	*Vorrei ...,*	vo·*ray* ...
please.	*per favore.*	per fa·*vo*·re
a table for	*un tavolo per*	oon *ta*·vo·lo per
(four)	*(quattro)*	(*kwa*·tro)
the (non)smoking	*(non) fumatori*	(non) foo·ma·*to*·ree
section		

Do you have vegetarian food?
   Avete piatti vegetariani?   a·*ve*·te *pya*·tee ve·je·ta·*rya*·nee

What would you recommend?
   Cosa mi consiglia?   *ko*·za mee kon·*see*·lya

I'll have a ...	*Prendo ...*	*pren*·do ...
Cheers!	*Salute!*	sa·*loo*·te

I'd like (the) ...,	Vorrei ...,	vo·ray ...
please.	per favore.	per fa·vo·re
bill	il conto	eel kon·to
menu	il menù	eel me·noo
that dish	questo piatto	kwe·sto pya·to
(cup of) coffee/tea	(un) caffè/tè	(oon) ka·fe/te

Would you like a drink?
Prendi qualcosa da bere?
pren·dee kwal·ko·za da be·re

(mineral) water	acqua (minerale)	a·kwa (mee·ne·ra·le)
bottle of (beer)	una bottiglia	oo·na bo·tee·lya
	di (birra)	dee (bee·ra)
glass of (wine)	un bicchiere	oon bee·kye·re
	di (vino)	dee (vee·no)
breakfast	prima colazione	pree·ma ko·la·tsyo·ne
lunch	pranzo	pran·dzo
dinner	cena	che·na

Italian

exploring

Where's the ...?	Dov'è ...?	do·ve ...
bank	la banca	la ban·ka
hotel	l'albergo	lal·ber·go
post office	l'ufficio postale	loo·fee·cho pos·ta·le

Can you show me (on the map)?
Può mostrarmi (sulla pianta)?   pwo mos·trar·mee (soo·la pyan·ta)

What time does it open/close?
A che ora apre/chiude?   a ke o·ra a·pre/kyoo·de

What's the admission charge?
Quant'è il prezzo d'ingresso?   kwan·te eel pre·tso deen·gre·so

When's the next tour?
A che ora parte la   a ke o·ra par·te la
prossima gita turistica?   pro·see·ma jee·ta too·ree·stee·ka

Where can I find ...?	*Dove sono ...?*	do·ve so·no ...
clubs	*dei clubs*	day kloob
gay venues	*dei locali gay*	day lo·ka·lee ge
pubs	*dei pub*	day pab

Can we get there by public transport?

Possiamo andare lì con i mezzi pubblici? — pos·ya·mo an·da·re lee kon ee me·tsee poob·lee·chee

Where can I buy a ticket?

Dove posso comprare un biglietto? — do·ve po·so kom·pra·re oon bee·lye·to

One ... ticket (to Rome), please.	*Un biglietto ... (per Roma), per favore.*	oon bee·lye·to ... (per ro·ma), per fa·vo·re
one-way	*di sola andata*	dee so·la an·da·ta
return	*di andata e ritorno*	dee an·da·ta e ree·tor·no

My luggage has been ...	*Il mio bagaglio è stato ...*	eel mee·o ba·ga·lyo e sta·to ...
lost	*perso*	per·so
stolen	*rubato*	roo·ba·to

Is this the ... to (Venice)?	*È questo/questa ... per (Venezia)?* m/f	e kwes·to/kwes·ta ... per (ve·ne·tsya)
boat	*la nave* f	la na·ve
bus	*l'autobus* m	low·to·boos
plane	*l'aereo* m	la·e·re·o
train	*il treno* m	eel tre·no

What time's the ... bus?	*A che ora passa ... autobus?*	a ke o·ra pa·sa ... ow·to·boos
first	*il primo*	eel pree·mo
last	*l'ultimo*	lool·tee·mo
next	*il prossimo*	eel pro·see·mo

I'd like a taxi ...	*Vorrei un tassì ...*	vo·ray oon ta·see ...
at (9am)	*alle (nove di mattina)*	a·le (no·ve dee ma·tee·na)
tomorrow	*domani*	do·ma·nee

How much is it to ...?
Quant'è per ...?   kwan-*te* per ...

Please take me to (this address).
Mi porti a (questo   mee *por*-tee a (*kwe*-sto
indirizzo), per piacere.   een-dee-*ree*-tso) per pya-*che*-re

Please stop here.
Si fermi qui, per favore.   see *fer*-mee kwee per fa-*vo*-re

shopping

Where's the (market)?	*Dov'è (il mercato)?*	do-*ve* (eel mer-*ka*-to)
I'm looking for ...	*Sto cercando ...*	sto cher-*kan*-do ...
It's faulty.	*È difettoso.*	e dee-fe-*to*-zo
I'd like ...,	*Vorrei ...,*	vo-*ray* ...
please.	*per favore.*	per fa-*vo*-re
a refund	*un rimborso*	oon reem-*bor*-so
to return this	*restituire*	res-tee-*twee*-re
	questo	*kwe*-sto

How much is it?
Quant'è?   kwan-*te*

Can you write down the price?
Può scrivere il prezzo?   pwo *skree*-ve-re eel *pre*-tso

That's too expensive.
È troppo caro.   e *tro*-po *ka*-ro

There's a mistake in the bill.
C'è un errore nel conto.   che oon e-*ro*-re nel *kon*-to

Do you accept ...?	*Accettate ...?*	a-che-*ta*-te ...
credit cards	*la carta di*	la *kar*-ta dee
	credito	*kre*-dee-to
travellers	*gli assegni*	lyee a-*se*-nyee
cheques	*di viaggio*	dee vee-*a*-jo
I'd like ...,	*Vorrei ...,*	vo-*ray* ...
please.	*per favore.*	per fa-*vo*-re
a receipt	*una ricevuta*	oo-na ree-che-*voo*-ta
my change	*il mio resto*	eel *mee*-o *res*-to

Italian

71

working

Where's the (business centre)?
Dov'è (il business centre)?   do·*ve* (eel *beez*·nees *sen*·ter)

I'm attending a ...	Sono qui per ...	so·no kwee per ...
conference	una conferenza	oo·na kon·fe·*ren*·tsa
course	un corso	oon *kor*·so
meeting	una riunione	oo·na ree·oo·*nyo*·ne
trade fair	una fiera	oo·na *fye*·ra
	commerciale	ko·mer·*cha*·le

I have an appointment with ...
Ho un appuntamento con ...   o oo·na·poon·ta·*men*·to kon ...

I'm with my colleagues.
Sono qui con i miei colleghi.   so·no kwee kon ee myay ko·*le*·gee

Here's my business card.
Ecco il mio biglietto da visita.   e·ko eel *mee*·o bee·*lye*·to da *vee*·zee·ta

That went very well.
È andato bene.   e an·*da*·to *be*·ne

emergencies

Help!	Aiuto!	ai·*yoo*·to
Stop!	Fermi!	*fer*·mee
Go away!	Vai via!	vai *vee*·a
Thief!	Ladro!	*la*·dro
Fire!	Al fuoco!	al *fwo*·ko

Call ...!	Chiami ...!	*kya*·mee ...
an ambulance	un'ambulanza	o·nam·boo·*lan*·tsa
a doctor	un medico	oon *me*·dee·ko
the police	la polizia	la po·lee·*tsee*·a

Could you help me, please?	Mi può aiutare, per favore?	mee pwo ai·yoo·*ta*·re per fa·*vo*·re
I'm lost.	Mi sono perso/a. m/f	mee *so*·no *per*·so/a
Where are the toilets?	Dove sono i gabinetti?	*do*·ve *so*·no ee ga·bee·*ne*·tee

72

Portuguese

Portugal's cities are life-affirming, lung-busting hotspots of hills, cafés and culture.

Pronunciation

Vowels		Consonants	
Symbol	**English sound**	**Symbol**	**English sound**
a	run	b	bed
aa	father	d	dog
ai	aisle	f	fat
ay	say	g	go
e	bet	k	kit
ee	see	l	lot
o	pot	ly	million
oh	oh	m	man
oo	book	n	not
ow	how	ng	ring (indicates the nasalisation of the preceding vowel)
oy	toy	ny	canyon

The Portuguese pronunciation is given in blue after each word or phrase. Read these words as though you were reading English and you're sure to be understood. Each syllable is separated by a dot, and italics indicate that you need to put stress on that syllable, for example:

De nada.   de *naa*·da

p	pet
r	like 'tt' in 'butter' said fast
rr	run (throaty)
s	sun
sh	shot
t	top
v	very
w	win
y	yes
z	zero
zh	pleasure

Portuguese

essentials

Yes/No.	Sim/Não.	seeng/nowng
Hello/Goodbye.	Olá/Adeus.	o-laa/a-de-oosh
Please.	Por favor.	poor fa-vor
Thank you (very much).	(Muito) Obrigado/a. m/f	(mweeng-too) o-bree-gaa-doo/a
You're welcome.	De nada.	de naa-da
Excuse me.	Faz favor.	faash fa-vor
Sorry.	Desculpe.	desh-kool-pe

Do you speak English?
Fala inglês?   faa-la eeng-glesh

Do you understand?
Entende?   eng-teng-de

I (don't) understand.
(Não) Entendo.   (nowng) eng-teng-doo

chatting

introductions

Mr	Senhor	se-nyor
Mrs/Ms	Senhora/Senhorita	se-nyo-ra/se-nyo-ree-ta
How are you?	Como está?	ko-moo shtaa
Fine. And you?	Bem. E você?	beng e vo-se
What's your name?	Qual é o seu nome?	kwaal e oo se-oo no-me
My name is ...	O meu nome é ...	oo me-oo no-me e ...
I'm pleased to meet you.	Prazer em conhecê-lo/ conhecê-la. m/f	pra-zer eng koo-nye-se-lo/ koo-nye-se-la
Here's my ...	Aqui está o meu ...	a-kee shtaa oo me-oo ...
What's your ...?	Qual é o seu ...?	kwaal e oo se-oo ...
address	endereço	eng-de-re-soo
email address	email	ee-mayl
phone number	número de telefone	noo-me-roo de te-le-fo-ne

75

What's your occupation?
Qual é a sua profissão?   kwaal e a *soo*·a proo·fee·*sowng*

I'm a ...   *Sou ...*   soh ...
   businessperson   *homem/mulher*   o·meng/moo·*lyer*
                        de negócios m/f   de ne·*go*·syoosh
   student   *estudante*   shtoo·*dang*·te

Where are you from?
De onde é?   dong·de e

I'm from (England).
Eu sou da (Inglaterra).   e·oo soh da (eeng·gla·*te*·rra)

Are you married?
É casado/a? m/f   e ka·*zaa*·doo/a

I'm married.
Eu sou casado/a. m/f   e·oo soh ka·*zaa*·doo/a

I'm single.
Eu sou solteiro/a. m/f   e·oo soh sol·*tay*·roo/a

How old are you?
Quantos anos tem?   kwang·toosh a·noosh teng

I'm ... years old.
Tenho ... anos.   ta·nyoo ... a·noosh

making conversation

What's the weather like?
Como está o tempo?   ko·moo shtaa oo *teng*·poo

It's ...   *Está ...*   shtaa ...
   cold   *frio*   free·oo
   hot   *muito quente*   mweeng·too keng·te
   raining   *a chover*   a shoo·ver
   snowing   *a nevar*   a ne·vaar

Do you live here?
Mora aqui?   mo·ra a·kee

Where are you going?
Onde vai?   ong·de vai

What are you doing?
O que é que está a fazer?   oo ke e ke shtaa a fa·zer

76

invitations

Would you like to go (for a) ...?	Gostava de ir ...?	goosh·*taa*·va de eer ...
dancing	*dançar*	dang·*saar*
drink	*beber alguma coisa*	be·*ber* aal·*goo*·ma *koy*·za
meal	*comer*	koo·*mer*
out	*sair*	sa·*eer*

Yes, I'd love to.
Sim, adorava. — seeng a·doo·*raa*·va

No, I'm afraid I can't.
Tenho muita pena, mas não posso. — *ta*·nyoo *mweeng*·ta *pe*·na mash nowng *po*·soo

I love it here!
Eu adoro!
e·oo a·*do*·roo

What time will we meet?
A que horas é que nos encontramos? — a ke *o*·rash e ke noosh eng·kong·*traa*·moosh

Where will we meet?
Onde é que nos encontramos? — *ong*·de e ke noosh eng·kong·*traa*·moosh

Let's meet at ...	Encontramo-nos ...	eng·kong·*traa*·moo·noosh ...
(eight) o'clock	*às (oito)*	aash (*oy*·too)
the entrance	*à entrada*	aa eng·*traa*·da

meeting up

Can I ...?	Posso ...?	*po*·soo ...
dance with you	*dançar contigo*	dang·*saar* kong·*tee*·goo
sit here	*sentar-me aqui*	seng·*taar*·me a·*kee*
take you home	*levar-te a casa*	le·*vaar*·te a *kaa*·za

77

I'm here with my girlfriend.
Estou aqui com a minha namorada.
shtoh a·*kee* kong a *mee*·nya na·moo·*raa*·da

I'm here with my boyfriend.
Estou aqui com o meu namorado.
shtoh a·*kee* kong oo *me*·oo na·moo·*raa*·doo

Keep in touch!
Mantenha-se em contacto!
mang·*te*·nya·se eng kong·*taak*·too

It's been great meeting you.
Foi fantástico conhecê-lo/conhecê-la. m/f
foy fang·*taash*·tee·koo koo·nye·*se*·loo/koo·nye·*se*·la

likes & dislikes

I thought it was ...	*Eu achei que ...*	e·oo a·*shay* ke ...
It's ...	*É ...*	e ...
awful	*horrível* m&f	o·*rree*·vel
great	*óptimo/óptima* m/f	*o*·tee·moo/*o*·tee·ma
interesting	*interessante* m&f	eeng·te·re·*sang*·te
Do you like ...?	*Gosta de ...?*	*gosh*·ta de ...
I (don't) like ...	*Eu (não) gosto de ...*	e·oo (nowng) *gosh*·too de ...
art	*arte*	*aar*·te
shopping	*ir às compras*	eer aash *kong*·prash
sport	*fazer desporto*	fa·*zer* desh·*por*·too

eating & drinking

I'd like ..., please.	*Queria uma ..., por favor.*	ke·*ree*·a *oo*·ma ... poor fa·*vor*
a table for (five)	*mesa para (cinco)*	*me*·za *pa*·ra (*seeng*·koo)
the (non)smoking section	*mesa de (não) fumador*	*me*·za de (nowng) foo·ma·*dor*

Do you have vegetarian food?
Tem comida vegetariana?
teng koo·*mee*·da ve·zhe·ta·ree·*aa*·na

What would you recommend?
O que é que recomenda?
oo ke e ke rre·koo·*meng*·da

I'll have a ...	*Eu queria ...*	*e·oo ke·ree·a ...*
Cheers!	*À nossa!*	aa *no*·sa
I'd like (the) ...,	*Queria ...,*	ke·*ree*·a ...
please.	*por favor.*	poor fa·*vor*
bill	*a conta*	a *kong*·ta
drink list	*a lista das*	a *leesh*·ta dash
	bebidas	be·*bee*·dash
menu	*um menu*	oong me·*noo*
that dish	*aquele prato*	a·*ke*·le *praa*·too

Would you like a drink?
Queres uma bebida?
ke·resh *oo*·ma be·*bee*·da

(cup of) coffee/tea	*(chávena de) café/chá*	(*shaa*·ve·na de) ka·*fe*/shaa
(mineral) water	*água (mineral)*	*aa*·gwa (mec·ne·*raal*)
bottle of (beer)	*uma garrafa*	*oo*·ma ga·*rraa*·fa
	de (cerveja)	de (ser·*ve*·zha)
glass of (wine)	*um copo de (vinho)*	oong *ko*·poo de (*vee*·nyoo)
breakfast	*pequeno almoço*	pe·*ke*·noo aal·*mo*·soo
lunch	*almoço*	aal·*mo*·soo
dinner	*jantar*	zhang·*taar*

exploring

Where's the ...?	*Onde é o ...?*	*ong*·de e oo ...
bank	*banco*	*bang*·koo
hotel	*hotel*	o·*tel*
post office	*correio*	koo·*rray*·oo

Can you show me (on the map)?
Pode-me mostrar (no mapa)? po·de·me moosh·*traar* (noo *maa*·pa)

What time does it open/close?
A que horas abre/fecha? a ke o·rash *aa*·bre/*fe*·sha

What's the admission charge?
Qual é o preço de entrada? kwaal e oo *pre*·soo de eng·*traa*·da

Portuguese

When's the next tour?

Quando é a próxima excursão?	kwang·doo e a pro·see·ma shkoor·sowng	

Where can I find …?   *Onde é que há …?*   ong·de e ke aa …

clubs	*discotecas*	deesh·koo·te·kash
gay venues	*lugares de gays*	loo·gaa·resh de gaysh
pubs	*bares*	ba·resh

Can we get there by public transport?

Podemos receber aí por transportes públicos?   poo·de·moosh rre·se·ber a·ee poor trangsh·por·tesh poo·blee·koosh

Where can I buy a ticket?

Onde é que eu compro o bilhete?   ong·de e ke e·oo kong·proo oo bee·lye·te

One … ticket (to Braga), please.	*Um bilhete de … (para Braga), por favor.*	oong bee·lye·te de … (pra braa·ga) poor fa·vor
one-way	*ida*	ee·da
return	*ida e volta*	ee·da ee vol·ta

My luggage has been …	*A minha bagagem …*	a mee·nya ba·gaa·zheng …
lost	*perdeu-se*	per·de·oo·se
stolen	*foi roubada*	foy rroh·baa·da

Is this the … to (Lisbon)?	*Este é o … para (Lisboa)?*	esh·te e oo … pra (leezh·bo·a)
boat	*barco*	baar·koo
bus	*autocarro*	ow·to·kaa·rroo
plane	*avião*	a·vee·owng
train	*comboio*	kong·boy·oo

What time's the … bus?	*Quando é que sai o … autocarro?*	kwang·doo e ke sai oo … ow·to·kaa·rroo
first	*primeiro*	pree·may·roo
last	*último*	ool·tee·moo
next	*próximo*	pro·see·moo

I'd like a taxi …	*Queria chamar um táxi …*	ke·ree·a sha·maar oong taak·see …
at (9am)	*para as (nove da manhã)*	pra ash (no·ve da ma·nyang)
tomorrow	*amanhã*	aa·ma·nyang

How much is it to ...?
Quanto custa até ao ...? kwang·too koosh·ta a·te ow ...

Please take me to (this address).
Leve-me para (este endereço), le·ve·me pa·ra (esh·te eng·de·re·soo)
por favor. poor fa·vor

Please stop here.
Por favor pare aqui. poor fa·vor paa·re a·kee

shopping

Where's the (market)?	Onde é (o mercado)?	ong·de e (oo mer·kaa·doo)
I'm looking for ...	Estou à procura de ...	shtoh aa proo·koo·ra de ...
It's faulty.	Tem defeito.	teng de·fay·too

I'd like ..., please. *Queria ..., por fuvor.* ke·rec·a ... poor fa·vor
   a refund *ser reembolsado/a* m/f ser rre·eng·bol·saa·doo/a
   to return this *devolver isto* de·vol·ver eesh·too

How much is it?
Quanto custa? kwang·too koosh·ta

Can you write down the price?
Pode escrever o preço? po·de shkre·ver oo pre·soo

That's too expensive.
Está muito caro. shtaa mweeng·too kaa·roo

There's a mistake in the bill.
Há um erro na conta. aa oong e·rroo na kong·ta

Do you accept ...? *Aceitam ...?* a·say·tang ...
   credit cards *cartão de crédito* kar·towng de kre·dee·too
   travellers cheques *travellers cheques* tra·ve·ler she·kesh

I'd like ..., please. *Queria ..., por favor.* ke·ree·a ... poor fa·vor
   a receipt *um recibo* oong rre·see·boo
   my change *o troco* oo tro·koo

Portuguese

81

working

English	Portuguese	Pronunciation
I'm attending a ...	Estou a participar ...	shtoh a par·tee·see·paar ...
meeting	numa reunião	noo·ma rree·oo·nyowng
trade fair	numa feira de comércio	noo·ma fay·ra de koo·mer·syoo

Where's the (business centre)?
Onde é (o centro de negócios)?
ong·de e (oo seng·troo de ne·go·syoosh)

I have an appointment with ...
Tenho uma reunião marcada com ...
ta·nyoo oo·ma rree·oo·nyowng mar·kaa·da kong ...

I'm with my colleagues.
Estou com colegas de trabalho.
shtoh kong koo·le·gash de tra·baa·lyoo

Here's my business card.
Aqui está o meu cartão de visita.
a·kee shtaa oo me·oo kar·towng de vee·zee·ta

That went very well.
Correu tudo muito bem.
ko·rre·oo too·doo mweeng·too beng

emergencies

English	Portuguese	Pronunciation
Help!	Socorro!	soo·ko·rroo
Stop!	Stop!	stop
Go away!	Vá-se embora!	vaa·se eng·bo·ra
Thief!	Ladrão!	la·drowng
Fire!	Fogo!	fo·goo
Call ...!	Chame ...!	shaa·me ...
a doctor	um médico	oong me·dee·koo
an ambulance	uma ambulância	oo·ma ang·boo·lang·sya
the police	a polícia	a poo·lee·sya
Could you help me, please?	Pode ajudar, por favor?	po·de a·zhoo·daar poor fa·vor
I'm lost.	Estou perdido/a. m/f	shtoh per·dee·doo/a
Where are the toilets?	Onde é a casa de banho?	ong·de e a kaa·za de ba·nyoo

82

Spanish

> Sitting right on the Mediterranean, every square metre of Barcelona is vibrant and proud.

Pronunciation

Vowels		Consonants	
Symbol	English sound	Symbol	English sound
a	**run**	b	**b**ed
ai	**ai**sle	ch	**ch**eat
ay	**say**	d	**d**og
e	**bet**	f	**f**at
ee	**see**	g	**g**o
o	**pot**	k	**k**it
oo	**zoo**	kh	lo**ch** (guttural)
ow	**how**	l	**l**ot
oy	**toy**	ly	mi**lli**on
		m	**m**an
		n	**n**ot
		ny	ca**ny**on
		p	**p**et
		r	like 'tt' in 'bu**tt**er' said fast
		rr	**r**un (rolled)
		s	**s**un
		t	**t**op
		th	**th**in
		v	between 'v' and 'b'
		w	**w**in
		y	**y**es

The Spanish pronunciation is given in blue after each word or phrase. Read these words as though you were reading English and you're sure to be understood. Each syllable is separated by a dot, and italics indicate that you need to put stress on that syllable, for example:

Gracias.   gra·thyas

essentials

Yes/No.	*Sí/No.*	see/no
Hello/Goodbye.	*Hola/Adiós.*	o·la/a·*dyos*
Please.	*Por favor.*	por fa·*vor*
Thank you (very much).	*(Muchas) Gracias.*	(*moo*·chas) *gra*·thyas
You're welcome.	*De nada.*	de *na*·da
Excuse me.	*Perdón/Discúlpeme.*	per·*don*/dees·*kool*·pe·me
Sorry.	*Lo siento.*	lo *syen*·to
Do you speak English?	*¿Habla inglés?*	*ab*·la een·*gles*
Do you understand?	*¿Me entiende?*	me en·*tyen*·de
I (don't) understand.	*(No) Entiendo.*	(no) en·*tyen*·do

chatting

introductions

Mr	*Señor*	se·*nyor*
Mrs/Miss	*Señora/Señorita*	se·*nyo*·ra/se·nyo·*ree*·ta
How are you?	*¿Qué tal?*	ke tal
Fine, thanks.	*Bien, gracias.*	byen *gra*·thyas
And you?	*¿Y Usted/tú?* pol/inf	ee oos·*te*/too
What's your name?	*¿Cómo se llama Usted?* pol	*ko*·mo se *lya*·ma oos·*te*
	¿Cómo te llamas? inf	*ko*·mo te *lya*·mas
My name is ...	*Me llamo ...*	me *lya*·mo ...
I'm pleased to meet you.	*Mucho gusto.*	*moo*·cho *goos*·to
Here's my ...	*Éste/Ésta es mi ...* m/f	*es*·te/a es mee ...
What's your ...?	*¿Cuál es su/tu ...?* pol/inf	kwal es soo/too ...
(email) address	*dirección (de email)* f	dee·rek·*thyon* (de *ee*·mayl)
phone number	*número de teléfono* m	*noo*·me·ro de te·*le*·fo·no

85

What's your occupation?

¿A qué se dedica Usted? pol		a ke se de-*dee*-ka oos-*te*
¿A qué te dedicas? inf		a ke te de-*dee*-kas

I'm a ... *Soy un/una ...* m/f soy oon/*oo*-na ...

businessperson	*comerciante*	ko-mer-*thyan*-te
student	*estudiante*	es-too-*dyan*-te

Where are you from?

¿De dónde es Usted? pol	de *don*-de es oos-*te*
¿De dónde eres? inf	de *don*-de e-res

I'm from (England).

Soy de (Inglaterra). soy de (een-gla-*te*-rra)

Are you married?

¿Está Usted casado/a? m/f pol	es-*ta* oos-*te* ka-*sa*-do/a
¿Estás casado/a? m/f inf	es-*tas* ka-*sa*-do/a

I'm married.

Estoy casado/a. m/f es-*toy* ka-*sa*-do/a

I'm single.

Soy soltero/a. m/f soy sol-*te*-ro/a

How old are you?

¿Cuántos años tiene Usted? pol	*kwan*-tos *a*-nyos *tye*-ne oos-*te*
¿Cuántos años tienes? inf	*kwan*-tos *a*-nyos *tye*-nes

I'm ... years old.

Tengo ... años. *ten*-go ... *a*-nyos

making conversation

What's the weather like?

¿Qué tiempo hace? ke *tyem*-po *a*-the

It's ...

cold	*Hace frío.*	*a*-the *free*-o
hot	*Hace calor.*	*a*-the ka-*lor*
raining	*Está lloviendo.*	es-*ta* lyo-*vyen*-do
snowing	*Está nevando.*	es-*ta* ne-*van*-do

Do you live here?

¿Vives aquí? *vee*-ves a-*kee*

Where are you going?
¿Adónde vas?   a·*don*·de vas

What are you doing?
¿Qué haces?   ke *a*·thes

invitations

Would you like	*¿Quieres que*	kye·res ke
to go (for a) ...?	*vayamos a ...?*	va·*ya*·mos a ...
dancing	*bailar*	bai·*lar*
drink	*tomar algo*	to·*mar* al·go
meal	*comer*	ko·*mer*
out	*salir*	sa·*leer*

Yes, I'd love to.
Me encantaría.   me en·kan·ta·*ree*·a

No, I'm afraid I can't.
Lo siento pero no puedo.   lo *syen*·to pe·ro no *pwe*·do

I love it here!
Me encanta aquí!
me en·*kan*·ta a·*kee*

What time shall we meet?
¿A qué hora quedamos?   a ke *o*·ra ke·*du*·mos

Where will we meet?
¿Dónde quedamos?   *don*·de ke·*da*·mos

Let's meet ...	*Quedamos ...*	ke·*da*·mos ...
at (eight) o'clock	*a (las ocho)*	a (las *o*·cho)
at the entrance	*en la entrada*	en la en·*tra*·da

meeting up

Can I ...?	*Puedo ...?*	*pwe*·do ...
dance with you	*bailar contigo*	bai·*lar* kon·*tee*·go
sit here	*sentarme aquí*	sen·*tar*·me a·*kee*
take you home	*llevarte a*	lye·*var*·te a
	tu casa	too *ka*·sa

I'm here with my boyfriend/girlfriend.
Estoy aquí con mi novio/a. es·*toy* a·*kee* kon mee *no*·vyo/a

Keep in touch!
¡Nos mantendremos nos man·ten·*dre*·mos
en contacto! en kon·*tak*·to

It's been great meeting you.
Me ha encantado conocerte. me a en·kan·*ta*·do ko·no·*ther*·te

likes & dislikes

I thought it was ...	*Pensé que era ...*	pen·*se* ke e·ra ...
It's ...	*Es ...*	es ...
awful	*feo*	*fe*·o
great	*sensacional*	sen·sa·thyo·*nal*
interesting	*interesante·*	een·te·re·*san*·te
Do you like ...	*¿Le gusta ...?* pol	le *goos*·ta ...
	¿Te gusta ...? inf	te *goos*·ta ...
I (don't) like ...	*(No) Me gusta ...*	(no) me *goos*·ta ...
art	*el arte*	el *ar*·te
shopping	*ir de compras*	eer de *kom*·pras
sport	*el deporte*	el de·*por*·te

eating & drinking

I'd like ...,	*Quisiera ...,*	kee·*sye*·ra ...
please.	*por favor.*	por fa·*vor*
a table for (two)	*una mesa*	*oo*·na *me*·sa
	para (dos)	*pa*·ra (dos)
the (non)smoking	*(no) fumadores*	(no) foo·ma·*do*·res
section		

Do you have vegetarian food?
¿Tienen comida tye·nen ko·*mee*·da
vegetariana? ve·khe·ta·*rya*·na

What would you recommend?
¿Qué recomienda? ke rre·ko·*myen*·da

I'll have a ...	*Para mí ...*	*pa*·ra mee ...
Cheers!	*¡Salud!*	sa·*loo*

I'd like (the) ...	*Quisiera ...,*	kee-*sye*-ra ...
	por favor.	por fa-*vor*
bill	*la cuenta*	la *kwen*-ta
drink list	*la lista de bebidas*	la *lees*-ta de be-*bee*-das
menu	*el menú*	el me-*noo*
that dish	*ese plato*	e-se *pla*-to

Would you like a drink?
¿Te apetece una copa?
te a·pe·*te*·the *oo*·na *ko*·pa

(cup of) coffee/tea	*(taza de) café/té*	(*ta*-tha de) ka-*fe*/te
(mineral) water	*agua (mineral)*	*a*-gwa (mee-ne-*ral*)
bottle of (beer)	*una botella de (cerveza)*	*oo*-na bo-*te*-lya de (*ther*-ve-tha)
glass of (wine)	*una copa de (vino)*	*oo*-na *ko*-pa de (*vee*-no)
breakfast	*desayuno*	de-sa-*yoo*-no
lunch	*comida*	ko-*mee*-da
dinner	*almuerzo*	al-*mwer*-tho

Spanish

exploring

Where's the ...?	*¿Dónde está el ...?*	*don*-de es-*ta* el ...
bank	*banco*	*ban*-ko
hotel	*hotel*	o-*tel*
post office	*correos*	ko-*rre*-os

Can you show me (on the map)?
¿Me lo puede indicar (en el mapa)? me lo *pwe*-de een-dee-*kar* (en el *ma*-pa)

What time does it open/close?
¿A qué hora abren/cierran? a ke *o*-ra *ab*-ren/*thye*-rran

What's the admission charge?
¿Cuánto cuesta la entrada? *kwan*-to *kwes*-ta la en-*tra*-da

When's the next tour?
¿Cuándo es el próximo recorrido? *kwan*-do es el *prok*-see-mo rre-ko-*rree*-do

Where can I find ...?	¿Dónde hay ...?	don·de ai ...
clubs	clubs nocturnos	kloobs nok·toor·nos
gay venues	lugares gay	loo·ga·res gai
pubs	bares	ba·res

Can we get there by public transport?

¿Podemos llegar ahí por transporte publico?	po·de·mos lye·gar a·ee por tran·spor·te poob·lee·ko

Where can I buy a ticket?

¿Dónde puedo comprar un billete?	don·de pwe·do kom·prar oon bee·lye·te

One ... ticket to (Barcelona), please.	Un billete ... a (Barcelona), por favor.	oon bee·lye·te ... a (bar·the·lo·na) por fa·vor
one-way	sencillo	sen·thee·lyo a
return	de ida y vuelta	de ee·da ee vwel·ta

My luggage has been ...	Mis maletas han sido ...	mees ma·le·tas an see·do ...
lost	perdidas	per·dee·das
stolen	robadas	rro·ba·das

Is this the ... to (Valencia)?	¿Es el ... para (Valencia)?	es el ... pa·ra (va·len·thya)
boat	barco	bar·ko
bus	autobús	ow·to·boos
plane	avión	a·vyon
train	tren	tren

What time's the ... bus?	¿A qué hora es el ... autobús?	a ke o·ra es el ... ow·to·boos
first	primer	pree·mer
last	último	ool·tee·mo
next	próximo	prok·see·mo

I'd like a taxi ...	Quisiera un taxi ...	kee·sye·ra oon tak·see ...
at (9am)	a (las nueve de la mañana)	a (las nwe·ve de la ma·nya·na)
tomorrow	mañana	ma·nya·na

How much is it to ...?
¿Cuánto cuesta ir a ...?   kwan·to kwes·ta eer a ...

Please take me to (this address).
Por favor, lléveme a   por fa·vor lye·ve·me a
(esta dirección).   (es·ta dee·rek·thyon)

Please stop here.
Por favor pare aquí.   por fa·vor pa·re a·kee

shopping

Where's the (market)?	*¿Dónde está (el mercado)?*	don·de es·ta (el mer·ka·do)
I'm looking for ...	*Estoy buscando ...*	es·toy boos·kan·do ...
It's faulty.	*Es defectuoso.*	es de·fek·too·o·so
I'd like ..., please.	*Quisiera ..., por favor.*	kee·sye·ra ... por fa·vor
a refund	*que me devuelva el dinero*	ke me de·vwel·va el dee·ne·ro
to return this	*devolver esto*	de·vol·ver es·to

How much is it?
¿Cuánto cuesta esto?   kwan·to kwes·ta es·to

Can you write down the price?
¿Puede escribir el precio?   pwe·de es·kree·beer el pre·thyo

That's too expensive.
Es muy caro.   es mooy ka·ro

There's a mistake in the bill.
Hay un error en la cuenta.   ai oon e·rror en la kwen·ta

Do you accept ...?	*¿Aceptan ...?*	a·thep·tan ...
credit cards	*tarjetas de crédito*	tar·khe·tas de kre·dee·to
travellers cheques	*cheques de viajero*	che·kes de vya·khe·ro
I'd like ..., please.	*Quisiera ..., por favor.*	kee·sye·ra ... por fa·vor
a receipt	*un recibo*	oon rre·thee·bo
my change	*mi cambio*	mee kam·byo

91

working

I'm attending a ...	Asisto a ...	a-sees-to a ...
conference	un congreso	oon kon-gre-so
course	un curso	oon koor-so
meeting	una reunión	oo-na re-oo-nyon
trade fair	una feria de	oo-na fe-rya de
	muestras	mwes-tras

Where's the (business centre)?
¿Dónde está (el centro   *don-*de es-*ta* (el *then-*tro
financiero)?   fee-nan-*thye-*ro)

I have an appointment with ...
Tengo una cita con ...   *ten-*go oo-na *thee-*ta kon ...

I'm with my colleagues.
Estoy con mis colegas.   es-*toy* kon mees ko-*le-*gas

Here's my business card.
Aquí tiene mi tarjeta   a-*kee* tye-ne mee tar-*khe-*ta
de visita.   de vee-*see-*ta

That went very well.
Eso fue muy bien.   e-so fwe mooy byen

emergencies

Help!	¡Socorro!	so-ko-ro
Stop!	¡Pare!	pa-re
Go away!	¡Váyase!	va-ya-se
Thief!	¡Ladrón!	lad-ron
Fire!	¡Fuego!	fwe-go

Call ...!	¡Llame a ...!	lya-me a ...
an ambulance	una ambulancia	oo-na am-boo-lan-thya
a doctor	un médico	oon me-dee-ko
the police	la policía	la po-lee-thee-a

Could you help me,   *¿Me puede ayudar,*   me *pwe-*de a-yoo-*dar*
   please?   *por favor?*   por fa-*vor*
I'm lost.   *Estoy perdido/a.* m/f   es-*toy* per-*dee-*do/a
Where are   *¿Dónde están*   *don-*de es-*tan*
   the toilets?   *los servicios?*   los ser-*vee-*thyos

Swedish

"
The dream of a blonde populace enjoying a fabulously high standard of living is not too far from the truth.
"

Pronunciation

Vowels		Consonants	
Symbol	**English sound**	**Symbol**	**English sound**
a	run	b	bed
aa	father	ch	cheat
ai	aisle	d	dog
aw	saw	f	fat
e	bet	fh	f pronounced with rounded lips
air	hair	g	go
ee	see	h	hat
eu	nurse	k	kit
ew	ee pronounced with rounded lips	l	lot
ey	as in 'bet', but longer	m	man
i	hit	n	not
o	pot	ng	ring
oh	oh	p	pet
oo	zoo	r	red
u	put	s	sun
		sh	shot
		t	top
		v	very
		y	yes

The Swedish pronunciation is given in blue after each word or phrase. Read these words as though you were reading English and you're sure to be understood. Each syllable is separated by a dot, and italics indicate that you need to put stress on that syllable, for example:

Ursäkta mig.   oor-*shek*·ta mey

essentials

Yes/No.	*Ja/Nej.*	yaa/ney
Hello/Goodbye.	*Hej/Adjö.*	hey/aa-*yeu*
Please.	*Tack.*	tak
Thank you (very much).	*Tack (så mycket).*	tak (saw *mew*-ke)
You're welcome.	*Varsågod.*	var-sha-*gohd*
Excuse me.	*Ursäkta mig.*	oor-*shek*-ta mey
Sorry.	*Förlåt.*	feur-*lawt*

Do you speak English?
  Talar du engelska?   taa-lar doo eng-el-ska

Do you understand?
  Förstår du?   feur-*shtawr* doo

I (don't) understand.
  Jag förstår (inte).   yaa feur-*shtawr* (*in*-te)

chatting

introductions

Mr	*herr*	her
Mrs/Miss	*fru/fröken*	froo/*freu*-ken

How are you?	*Hur står det till?*	hoor stawr de til
Fine, thanks.	*Bra, tack.*	braa tak
And you?	*Och dig?*	o dey
What's your name?	*Vad heter du?*	vaad *hey*-ter doo
My name is ...	*Jag heter ...*	yaa *hey*-ter ...
I'm pleased to meet you.	*Trevligt att träffas.*	*treyv*-lit at *tre*-fas

Here's my (email) address.
  Här är min (e-post) adress.   hair air min (*ey*-post) a-*dres*

What's your (email) address?
  Vad är din (e-post) adress?   vaad air din (*ey*-post) a-*dres*

Here's my phone number.
Här är mitt telefonnummer.   hair air mit te·le·*fohn*·nu·mer

What's your phone number?
Vad är ditt telefonnummer?   vaad air dit te·le·*fohn*·nu·mer

What's your occupation?
Vad har du för yrke?   vaad har doo feur *ewr*·ke

I'm a ...	*Jag är ...*	yaa air ...
businessperson	*affärsman*	a·*fairsh*·man
student	*studerande*	stu·*dey*·ran·de

Where are you from?
Varifrån kommer du?   var·ee·frawn *ko*·mer doo

I'm from (England).
Jag kommer från (England).   yaa *ko*·mer frawn (*eng*·land)

Are you married?
Är du gift?   air doo yift

I'm married/single.
Jag är gift/ogift.   yaa air yift/*oh*·yift

How old are you?
Hur gammal är du?   hoor *ga*·mal air doo

I'm ... years old.
Jag är ... år gammal.   yaa air ... awr *ga*·mal

making conversation

What's the weather like?
Hur är vädret?   hur air *vey*·dret

It's...		
cold	*Det är kallt.*	de air kalt
hot	*Det är hett.*	de air het
raining	*Det regnar.*	de *reng*·nar
snowing	*Det snöar.*	de *sneu*·ar

Do you live here?	*Bor du här?*	bor doo hair
Where are you going?	*Vart går du?*	vaart gawr doo
What are you doing?	*Vad gör du?*	vaad yeur doo

invitations

Would you like to go (for a) ...?	*Vill du gå ut ...?*	vil doo gaw oot ...
dancing	*och dansa*	o *dan*·sa
drink	*och ta en drink*	o taa eyn drink
meal	*och äta*	o *air*·ta
out somewhere	*någonstans*	*nawn*·stans

Yes, I'd love to.
Ja, gärna. yaa *yair*·na

No, I'm afraid I can't.
Nej, tyvärr kan jag inte. ney tew·*vair* kan yaa *in*·te

I love it here!
Jag gillar att vara här!
yaa *yi*·lar at *vaa*·ra hair

What time will we meet?
Hur dags ska vi träffas? hoor daks ska vee *tre*·fas

Where will we meet?
Var ska vi träffas? var ska vee *tre*·fas

Let's meet at ...	*Ska vi träffas ...?*	ska vee *tre*·fas ...
(eight) o'clock	*klockan (åtta)*	*klo*·kan (*aw*·ta)
the entrance	*vid ingången*	veed *in*·gawng·en

meeting up

Can I ...?	*Får jag ...?*	fawr yaa ...
dance with you	*dansa med dig*	*dan*·sa mey dey
sit here	*sitta här*	*si*·ta hair
take you home	*ta dig hem*	taa dey hem

I'm here with my girlfriend/boyfriend.
Jag är här med min yaa air hair meyd min
flickvän/pojkvän. *flik*·ven/*poyk*·ven

Keep in touch!
Hör av dig!　　　　　　　　　　heur aav dey

It's been great meeting you.
Trevligt att träffas.　　　　　　trey·vlit at tre·fas

likes & dislikes

I thought it	Jag tyckte att	yaa tewk·te at
was ...	det var ...	de var ...
It's ...	Det är ...	de air ...
awful	hemskt	hemskt
great	utmärkt	oot·mairkt
interesting	interessant	in·te·re·sant
Do you like ...?	Tycker du om ...?	tew·ker doo om ...
I (don't) like ...	Jag tycker (inte)	yaa tew·ker (in·te)
	om ...	om ...
art	konst	konst
shopping	att shoppa	at sho·pa
sport	sport	sport

eating & drinking

I'd like ...,	... , tack.	... tak
please.		
a table for	Ett bord för	et bord feur
(four)	(fyra)	(few·ra)
the nonsmoking	Rökfria	reuk·free·a
section	avdelningen	aav·del·ning·en
the smoking	Rökavdelningen	reuk·aav·del·ning·en
section		

Do you have vegetarian food?
Har ni vegetarisk mat?　　　　har nee ve·ge·taa·risk maat

What would you recommend?
Vad skulle ni anbefalla?　　　　vaad sku·le nee an·be·fa·la

I'll have a ...	Jag vill ha ...	yaa vil haa ...
Cheers!	Skål!	skawl

I'd like (the) ...	*Jag skulle vilja ha ...*	yaa *sku·le vil·ya haa ...*
bill	*räkningen*	*reyk·*ning·en
drink list	*dricklistan*	*driks·*lis·tan
menu	*menyn*	me·*newn*
that dish	*den maträtt*	deyn *maat·*ret

Would you like a drink?
Vill du ha en drink?
vil doo haa eyn drink

(cup of) coffee/tea	*(en kopp) kaffe/te*	(eyn kop) *ka·*fe/tey
(mineral) water	*(mineral)vatten*	(mi·ne·*raal·*)va·ten
bottle of (beer)	*en flaska (öl)*	eyn *flas·*ka (eul)
glass of (wine)	*ett glas (vin)*	et glaas (veen)
breakfast	*frukost*	*froo·*kost
lunch	*lunch*	lunsh
dinner	*middag*	*mi·*daa

exploring

Where's the ...?	*Var ligger ...?*	var *li·*ger ...
bank	*banken*	*ban·*ken
hotel	*hotellet*	hoh·*te·*let
post office	*posten*	*pos·*ten

Can you show me (on the map)?
Kan du visa mig (på kartan)?
kan doo *vee·*sa mey (paw *kar·*tan)

What time does it open/close?
Hur dags öppnar/stänger de?
hoor daks *eup·*nar/*steng·*ar dom

What's the admission charge?
Hur mycket kostar det i inträde?
hoor *mew·*ke *kos·*tar de i *in·*trey·de

When's the next tour?
När avgår nästa turen?
nair *aav·*gawr *nes·*ta *too·*ren

99

Where can I find ...?	*Var finns ...?*	var fins ...
clubs	*klubbarna*	klu·bar·na
gay venues	*gayklubbarna*	gay·klu·bar·na
pubs	*pubbarna*	pu·bar·na

Can we get there by public transport?

Kan vi åka dit med	kan vee aw·ka deet meyd
lokaltrafik?	loh·kaal·tra·feek

Where can I buy a ticket?

Var kan jag köpa en biljett?	var kan yaa sheu·pa eyn bil·yet

One ... ticket (to Stockholm), please.	*Jag skulle vilja ha en ... (till Stockholm).*	yaa sku·le vil·ya haa eyn ... (til stok·holm)
one-way	*enkelbiljett*	en·kel·bil·yet
return	*returbiljett*	re·toor·bil·yet

My luggage has been ...	*Mit bagage är blivit ...*	mit ba·gaash air blee·vit ...
lost	*förlorat*	feur·loh·rat
stolen	*stulit*	stoo·lit

Is this the ... to (Stockholm)?	*Är den här ... till (Stockholm)?*	air den hair ... til (stok·holm)
boat	*båten*	baw·ten
bus	*bussen*	bu·sen

Is this the ... to (Stockholm)?	*Är det här ... till (Stockholm)?*	air de hair ... til (stok·holm)
plane	*planet*	plaa·net
train	*tåget*	taw·get

What time's the ... bus?	*När går ...?*	nair gawr ...
first	*första bussen*	feursh·ta bu·sen
last	*sista bussen*	sis·ta bu·sen
next	*nästa buss*	nes·ta bus

I'd like a taxi ...	*Jag vill gärna få en taxi ...*	yaa vil yair·na faw eyn tak·see ...
at (9am)	*klockan (nio på morgonen)*	klo·kan (nee·oh paw mo·ro·nen)
tomorrow	*imorgon*	ee·mo·ron

How much is it to …?
   Vad kostar det till …?   vaad *kos*·tar de til …

Please take me to (this address).
   Kan du köra mig till   kan doo *sheu*·ra mey til
   (denna address)?   (*dey*·na a·*dres*)

Please stop here.
   Kan du stanna här?   kan doo *sta*·na *hair*

shopping

Where's the (market)?	Var ligger (salutorget)?	var *li*·ger (*saa*·loo·*tor*·yet)
I'm looking for …	Jag letar efter …	yaa *ley*·tar *ef*·ter …
It's faulty.	Den är felaktig.	deyn air *fey*·lak·ti
I'd like …, please.	Jag vill gärna …	yaa vil *yair*·na …
a refund	få en	faw eyn
	återbäring	*aw*·ter·bai·ring
to return this	återlämna	*aw*·ter·lem·na
	denna	*dey*·na

How much is it?
   Hur mycket kostar det?   hoor *mew*·ke *kos*·tar de

Can you write down the price?
   Kan du skriva ner priset?   kan du *skree*·va neyr *pree*·set

That's too expensive.
   Det är för dyrt.   de air feur dewrt

There's a mistake in the bill.
   Det är ett fel på räkningen.   de air et *fel* paw *reyk*·ning·en

I need a film for this camera.
   Jag skulle vilja ha en film   yaa *sku*·le *vil*·ya *haa* eyn film
   till den här kameran.   til deyn hair *kaa*·me·ra

Do you accept …?	Tar ni …?	tar nee …
credit cards	kreditkort	kre·*deet*·kort
travellers cheques	resecheckar	*rey*·se·she·kar

I'd like …, please.	Jag vill gärna ha …	yaa vil *yair*·na ha …
a receipt	ett kvitto	et *kvi*·to
my change	min växel	min *vek*·sel

working

Where's the (business centre)?
Var är (affärsecentret)? var air (a-*fairsh*-sent-tret)

I'm attending a ... *Jag deltar i ...* yaa *del*-tar ee ...
   conference *konferens* kon-fe-*rens*
   course *en kurs* en koosh
   meeting *ett möte* et *meu*-te

I'm visiting a trade fair.
Jag går på handelsmässa. yaa gawr paw han-dels-*me*-sa

I have an appointment with ...
Jag har en tidsbeställning yaa har eyn *teeds*-be-stel-ning
med ... mey ...

I'm with my colleagues.
Jag är här med mina kollegor. yaa air hair mey *mee*-na ko-*ley*-gor

Here's my business card.
Här är mitt affärskort. hair air mit a-*fairsh*-kort

That went very well.
Det gick mycket bra. dey yik *mew*-ke braa

emergencies

Help! *Hjälp!* yelp
Stop! *Stanna!* *sta*-na
Go away! *Försvinn!* feur-*shvin*
Thief! *Ta fast tjuven!* ta fast *shoo*-ven
Fire! *Elden är lös!* *el*-den air leus

Call ...! *Ring ...!* ring ...
   an ambulance *efter en ambulans* *ef*-ter en am-boo-*lans*
   a doctor *efter en doktor* *ef*-ter en *dok*-tor
   the police *polisen* poh-*lee*-sen

Could you help me, please? *Kan du hjälpa mig?* kan doo *yel*-pa mai
I'm lost. *Jag har gått vilse.* yaa har got *vil*-se
Where are the toilets? *Var är toaletten?* var air toh-aa-*le*-ten

Turkish

"
Without Turkey, the East and West may never have met.
"

Pronunciation

Vowels		Consonants	
Symbol	English sound	Symbol	English sound
a	**r**u**n**	b	**b**ed
ai	**ai**sle	ch	**ch**eat
ay	s**ay**	d	**d**og
e	b**e**t	f	**f**at
ee	s**ee**	g	**g**o
eu	n**ur**se	h	**h**at
ew	ee pronounced with rounded lips	j	**j**oke
o	p**o**t	k	**k**it
oo	z**oo**	l	**l**ot
uh	**a**go	m	**m**an
		n	**n**ot
		p	**p**et
		r	**r**ed (rolled)
		s	**s**un
		sh	**sh**ot
		t	**t**op
		v	**v**an (but softer, between 'v' and 'w')
		y	**y**es
		z	**z**ero
		zh	plea**s**ure

The Turkish pronunciation is given in blue after each word or phrase. Read these words as though you were reading English and you're sure to be understood. Each syllable is separated by a dot, and italics indicate that you need to put stress on that syllable, for example:

Lütfen.   *lewt*·fen

104

essentials

Yes/No.	*Evet/Hayır.*	e-*vet*/ha-*yuhr*
Hello/Goodbye.	*Merhaba/Hoşçakalın.*	mer-ha-ba/hosh-*cha*-ka-luhn
Please.	*Lütfen.*	*lewt*-fen
Thank you (very much).	*(Çok) Teşekkür ederim.*	(chok) te-shek-*kewr* e-*de*-reem
You're welcome.	*Birşey değil.*	beer-*shay* de-*eel*
Excuse me.	*Bakar mısınız?*	ba-*kar* muh-suh-*nuhz*
Sorry.	*Özür dilerim.*	eu-*zewr* dee-*le*-reem
Do you speak English?	*İngilizce konuşuyor musunuz?*	een-gee-*leez*-je ko-noo-*shoo* moo-soo-*nooz*
Do you understand?	*Anlıyor musun?*	an-*luh*-yor moo-*soon*
I understand.	*Anlıyorum.*	an-*luh*-yo-room
I don't understand.	*Anlamıyorum.*	an-*la* muh-yo-room

chatting

introductions

Mr	*Bay*	bai
Mrs/Miss	*Bayan*	ba-*yan*
How are you?	*Nasılsınız?*	na-suhl-suh-nuhz
Fine. And you?	*İyiyim. Ya siz?*	ee-*yee*-yeem ya seez
What's your name?	*Adınız nedir?*	a-duh-*nuhz* ne-deer
My name is ...	*Benim adım ...*	be-*neem* a-*duhm* ...
I'm pleased to meet you.	*Tanıştığımıza sevindim.*	ta-nuhsh-tuh-uh-muh-*za* se-veen-*deem*
Here's my ...	*İşte benim ...*	eesh-*te* be-*neem* ...
(email) address	*(e-posta) adresim*	(e-pos-ta) ad-re-*seem*
phone number	*telefon numaram*	te-le-*fon* noo-ma-*ram*
What's your ...?	*Sizin ... nedir?*	see-*zeen* ... ne-deer
(email) address	*(e-posta) adresiniz*	(e-pos-ta) ad-re-se-*neez*
phone number	*telefon numaranız*	te-le-*fon* noo-ma-ra-*nuhz*

What's your occupation?
Mesleğiniz nedir?   mes·le·ee·*neez* ne·deer

I'm a ...   *Ben ...*   ben ...
  businessperson   *iş adamıyım* m   ish a·da·*muh*·yuhm
                        kadınıyım f   ka·duh·*nuh*·yuhm
  student   *öğrenci*   eu·ren·*jee*

Where are you from?
Nerelisiniz?   ne·re·lee·see·neez

I'm from (England).
Ben (İngiltere'liyim).   ben (een·geel·*te*·re·lee·yeem)

Are you married?
Evli misiniz?   ev·*lee* mee·see·*neez*

I'm married/single.
Ben evliyim/bekarım.   ben ev·*lee*·yeem/be·*ka*·ruhm

How old are you?
Kaç yaşındasınız?   kach ya·shuhn·*da*·suh·nuhz

I'm ... years old.
Ben ... yaşındayım.   ben ... ya·shuhn·*da*·yuhm

making conversation

What's the weather like?
Hava nasıl?   ha·*va* na·suhl

It's ...   *Hava ...*   ha·*va* ...
  cold   *soğuk*   so·*ook*
  hot   *sıcak*   suh·*jak*
  raining   *yağmurlu*   ya·moor·*loo*
  snowing   *kar yağışlı*   kar ya·uhsh·*luh*

Do you live here?
Burada mı oturuyorsunuz?   boo·ra·*da* muh o·too·*roo*·yor·soo·nooz

Where are you going?
Nereye gidiyorsunuz?   ne·re·ye gee·*dee*·yor·soo·nooz

What are you doing?
Ne yapıyorsunuz?   ne ya·*puh*·yor·soo·nooz

invitations

Would you like to go (for a) ...?	... gitmek ister misin?	... geet-mek ees-ter mee-seen
dancing	Dansa	dan-sa
drink	Birşeyler içmeye	beer-shay-ler eech-me-ye
meal	Yemeğe	ye-me-e
out	Bir yere	beer ye-re

Yes, I'd love to.
Evet, çok sevinirim. e-vet chok se-vee-nee-reem

No, I'm afraid I can't.
Üzgünüm ama gelemem. ewz-gew-newm a-ma ge-le-mem

I love it here!
Ben burayı seviyorum!
ben boo-ra-yuh se-vee-yo-room

What time will we meet?
Saat kaçta buluşacağız? sa-at kach-ta boo-loo-sha-ja-uhz

Where will we meet?
Nerede buluşacağız? ne-re-de boo-loo-sha-ja-uhz

Let's meet at ...	... buluşalım.	... boo-loo-sha-luhm
(eight) o'clock	Saat (sekizde)	sa-at (se-keez-de)
the entrance	Girişte	gee-reesh-te

meeting up

Can I ...?	... miyim?	... mee-yeem
dance with you	Sizinle dans edebilir	see-zeen-le dans e-de-bee-leer
sit here	Buraya oturabilir	boo-ra-ya o-too-ra-bee-leer
take you home	Sizi eve bırakabilir	see-zee e-ve buh-ra-ka-bee-leer

I'm here with my girlfriend/boyfriend.
Kız/Erkek arkadaşımla buradayım. kuhz/er-kek ar-ka-da-shuhm-la boo-ra-da-yuhm

Keep in touch!
Haberleşelim.　　　　ha·ber·le·she·*leem*

It's been great meeting you.
Tanıştığımıza çok　　ta·nuhsh·tuh·uh·muh·*za* chok
memnun oldum.　　　mem·*noon* ol·*doom*

likes & dislikes

I thought it	*... olduğunu*	*... ol·doo·oo·noo*
was ...	*düşünüyorum.*	dew·shew·*new*·yo·room
It's ...	*O ...*	o ...
awful	*korkunç*	kor·*koonch*
great	*harika*	ha·ree·*ka*
interesting	*ilginç*	eel·*geench*
Do you like ...?	*... sever misin?*	... se·*ver* mee·*seen*
I like ...	*... seviyorum.*	... se·vee·yo·room
I don't like ...	*... sevmiyorum.*	... sev·mee·yo·room
art	*Sanat*	sa·*nat*
shopping	*Alış-veriş*	a·luhsh·ve·*reesh*
	yapmayı	yap·ma·*yuh*
sport	*Sporu*	spo·*roo*

(margin: Turkish)

eating & drinking

I'd like ..., please.	*... istiyorum.*	... ees·*tee*·yo·room
a table for (five)	*(Beş) kişilik*	(besh) kee·shee·*leek*
	bir masa	beer ma·*sa*
the nonsmoking	*Sigara*	see·*ga*·ra
section	*içilmeyen*	ee·*cheel*·me·yen
	bir yer	beer yer
the smoking	*Sigara içilen*	see·*ga*·ra ee·chee·*len*
section	*bir yer*	beer yer

Do you have vegetarian food?
Vejeteryan yiyecekleriniz　　ve·zhe·ter·*yan* yee·ye·jek·le·ree·*neez*
var mı?　　　　　　　　　var muh

What would you recommend?
Ne tavsiye edersiniz?　　ne tav·see·*ye* e·*der*·see·neez

I'll have ...	... *alayım.*	... a-la-*yuhm*
Cheers!	*Şerefe!*	she-re-*fe*

I'd like (a/the)...	... *istiyorum.*	... ees-*tee*-yo-room
bill	*Hesabı*	he-sa-*buh*
drink list	*İçecek listesini*	ee-che-*jek* lees-te-see-*nee*
menu	*Menüyü*	me-new-*yew*
that dish	*Şu yemeği*	shoo ye-me-*ee*

Would you like a drink?
Bir içki ister misiniz?
beer eech-*kee* ees-*ter* mee-see-*neez*

(cup of) coffee/tea	*(fincan) kahve/çay*	(feen-*jan*) kah-*ve*/chai
mineral water	*maden suyu*	ma-*den* soo-*yoo*
water	*su*	soo
bottle of (beer)	*bir şişe (bira)*	beer shee-*she* (*bee*-ra)
glass of (wine)	*bir bardak (şarap)*	beer bar-*dak* (sha-*rap*)
breakfast	*kahvaltı*	kah-val-*tuh*
lunch	*öğle yemeği*	eu-*le* ye-me-*ee*
dinner	*akşam yemeği*	ak-*sham* ye-me-*ee*

Turkish

exploring

Where's the ...?	... *nerede?*	... ne-re-de
bank	*Banka*	*ban*-ka
hotel	*Otel*	o-*tel*
post office	*Postane*	pos-*ta*-ne

Can you show me (on the map)?
Bana (haritada) ba-*na* (ha-ree-ta-*da*)
gösterebilir misiniz? geus-te-*re*-bee-leer mee-seen-*neez*

What time does it open/close?
Saat kaçta açılır/kapanır? sa-*at* kach-*ta* a-chuh-*luhr*/ka-pa-*nuhr*

What's the admission charge?
Giriş ücreti nedir? gee-*reesh* ewj-re-*tee* ne-*deer*

When's the next tour?
Sonraki tur ne zaman? son-ra-*kee* toor ne za-*man*

Where can I find ...?	*Buranın ...* *nerede?*	boo-ra-*nuhn* ... ne-re-de
clubs	*kulüpleri*	koo-lewp-le-*ree*
gay venues	*gey kulüpleri*	gay koo-lewp-le-*ree*
pubs	*birahaneleri*	bee-ra-ha-ne-le-*ree*

Can we get there by public transport?
Oraya toplu taşım aracı o-ra-*ya* top-*loo* ta-*shuhm* a-ra-*juh*
ile gidebilir miyiz? ee-*le* gee-de-bee-*leer* mee-*yeez*

Where can I buy a ticket?
Nereden bilet alabilirim? ne-re-den bee-*let* a-*la*-bee-lee-reem

One ... ticket to (Bostancı), please.	*(Bostancı'ya) ...* *lütfen.*	(bos-*tan*-juh-ya) ... *lewt*-fen
one-way	*bir gidiş* *bileti*	beer gee-*deesh* bee-le-*tee*
return	*gidiş-dönüş* *bir bilet*	gee-deesh-deu-*newsh* beer bee-*let*

My luggage has been ...	*Bagajım ...*	ba-ga-*zhuhm* ...
lost	*kayboldu*	kai-bol-*doo*
stolen	*çalındı*	cha-luhn-*duh*

Is this the ... to (Sirkeci)?	*(Sirkeci'ye) giden* *... bu mu?*	(seer-ke-jee-ye) gee-den ... boo moo
boat	*vapur*	va-*poor*
bus	*otobüs*	o-to-*bews*
plane	*uçak*	oo-*chak*
train	*tren*	tren

What time's the ... bus?	*... otobüs* *ne zaman?*	... o-to-*bews* ne za-*man*
first	*İlk*	eelk
last	*Son*	son
next	*Sonraki*	son-ra-*kee*

I'd like a taxi ...	*... bir taksi* *istiyorum.*	... beer tak-*see* ees-*tee*-yo-room
at (9am)	*(Sabah dokuzda)*	(sa-*bah* do-kooz-*da*)
tomorrow	*Yarın*	*ya*-ruhn

How much is it to ...?
... ne kadar? ... ne ka-*dar*

110

Please take me to (this address).

Lütfen beni (bu adrese)	*lewt·fen be·nee* (boo ad·re·se)
götürün.	geu·tew·rewn

Please stop here.

Lütfen burada durun.	*lewt·fen* boo·ra·da doo·roon

shopping

Where's the (market)?	*(Pazar yeri) nerede?*	*(pa·zar ye·ree) ne·re·de*
I'm looking for ...	*... istiyorum.*	*... ees·tee·yo·room*
It's faulty.	*Arızalı.*	a·ruh·za·luh
I'd like ..., please.	*... istiyorum lütfen.*	*... ees·tee·yo·room lewt·fen*
a refund	*Para iadesi*	pa·ra ee·a·de·see
to return this	*Bunu iade etmek*	boo·noo ee·a·de et·mek

How much is it?

Ne kadar?	ne ka·dar

Can you write down the price?

Fiyatı yazabilir misiniz?	fee·ya·tuh ya·za·bee·leer mee·see·neez

That's too expensive.

Bu çok pahalı.	boo chok pa·ha·luh

There's a mistake in the bill.

Hesapta bir yanlışlık var.	he·sap·ta beer yan·luhsh·luhk var

I need a film for this camera.

Bu kamera için film istiyorum.	boo ka·me·ra ee·cheen feelm ees·tee·yo·room

Do you accept ...?	*... kabul ediyor musunuz?*	*... ka·bool e·dee·yor moo·soo·nooz*
credit cards	*Kredi kartı*	kre·dee kar·tuh
travellers cheques	*Seyahat çeki*	se·ya·hat che·kee
I'd like ..., please.	*... istiyorum lütfen.*	*... ees·tee·yo·room lewt·fen*
a receipt	*Makbuz*	mak·booz
my change	*Paramın üstünü*	pa·ra·muhn ews·tew·new

Turkish

111

working

Where's the (business centre)?
(İş merkezi) nerede?   (eesh mer·ke·*zee*) ne·re·de

I'm attending a ...   *Bir ... katılıyorum.*   beer ... ka·tuh·*luh*·yo·room
    conference   *konferansa*   kon·fe·ran·*sa*
    course   *kursa*   koor·*sa*
    meeting   *toplantıya*   top·lan·tuh·*ya*
    trade fair   *ticaret fuarına*   tee·ja·*ret* foo·a·ruh·*na*

I have an appointment with ...
... ile randevum var.   ... ee·*le* ran·de·*voom* var

I'm with my colleagues.
İş arkadaşlarımla   eesh ar·ka·dash·la·*ruhm*·la
birlikteyim.   beer·leek·*te*·yeem

Here's my business card.
Buyurun benim   boo·*yoo*·roon be·*neem*
kartvizitim.   kart·vee·zee·*teem*

That went very well.
Çok güzel geçti.   chok gew·*zel* gech·*tee*

emergencies

Help!	*İmdat!*	*eem*·dat
Stop!	*Dur!*	door
Go away!	*Git burdan!*	geet boor·*dan*
Thief!	*Hırsız var!*	huhr·*suhz* var
Fire!	*Yangın var!*	yan·*guhn* var
Call ...!	*... çağırın!*	... cha·*uh*·ruhn
an ambulance	*Ambulans*	am·boo·*lans*
a doctor	*Doktor*	dok·*tor*
the police	*Polis*	po·*lees*
Could you help me,	*Yardım edebilir*	yar·*duhm* e·*de*·bee·leer
please?	*misiniz lütfen?*	mee·see·*neez* lewt·fen
I'm lost.	*Kayboldum.*	kai·bol·*doom*
Where are the	*Tuvaletler nerede?*	too·va·let·*ler* ne·re·de
toilets?		

Turkish

24 hours
in the city

24 hours in the city

24 hours in the city? Hit the streets and savour every second . . .

Amsterdam

9am Be early to beat the crowds at the Anne Frank Huis and the Van Gogh Museum – two of Amsterdam's must-sees. But first, fuel up with a magnificent freshly-made breakfast at the window-lined Café Reibach in the Jordaan.

12pm For lunch try some delicious sweet or savoury pancakes in one of the typical pancake houses. Window-shop in the Negen Straatjes (Nine Alleys) district and be charmed by the many arty boutiques or peruse the funky shops, bohemian bars and hip galleries of the Jordaan, the city's working class stronghold.

3pm Claim a grassy stretch in the pleasant Vondelpark, or people-watch from the patio of the popular Round Blue Teahouse.

7pm Explore the (in)famous Red Light District, which is actually a very pretty part of town. Dine at the classic Dutch restaurant D'Vijff Vlieghen, then see the latest blockbuster at the magnificent Art Deco Tuschinskitheater; linger with the locals over a beer in a café or dance the night away at the Paradiso.

24 hours in the city

Athens

9am Have breakfast at Klepsidra, a cosy café that overlooks the picturesque Anafiotika quarter in Plaka, then head to the Acropolis and thrill at its crowning glory, the Parthenon.

12pm Stop for a home-style lunch under the giant plane tree at Platanos taverna, then take a stroll through Anafiotika's labyrinth of quiet, narrow paths with whitewashed Cycladic-style houses built by stonemasons from the island of Anafi.

3pm Walk through the Roman Agora and puzzle over the Tower of the Winds, which functions as a sundial, weather vane, water clock and compass. Later, check out the world's best collection of Greek antiquities at the National Archaeological Museum.

7pm Enjoy the spectacle of the changing of the guards at Parliament House in Syntagma before dining on the rooftop terrace of the Strofi taverna, which offers superb views of the illuminated Acropolis. End your day with a nightcap at a bar in lively Psiri.

Barcelona

7am Go for a stroll along Las Ramblas, one of the world's most beautiful city walks, and watch the street performers and florists set up for the day.

9am Retreat to the Café de l'Ópera and enjoy the sight of the arriving crowds. Hop on the metro and track down La Sagrada Família, Casa Batlló and Parc Güell – Gaudí's exuberant creations.

2pm Grab an outdoor table at the Plaça Reial and survey Gaudí's first tentative forays into architecture (in the form of lampposts). Head to the nearby Museu Picasso, pausing for another pit stop at the Plaça de Sant Josep Oriol, one of the Barri Gòtic's prettiest squares. Rejuvenate flagging energy levels with a walk along the beach.

10pm Hit El Born, one of Barcelona's coolest *barrios* (neighbourhoods). Its restaurants attract an offbeat crowd and the cosy bars are favourite evening haunts of local people – you'll be tempted to stay out until the morning.

24 hours in the city

Berlin

11am Do what Berlin does and wake up mid-morning. Then grab a table in the sun at Cafe Berio in Schöneberg. As you enjoy your leisurely breakfast, watch the world on parade.

1pm Cross the sculpture-studded Schlossbrüke (Palace Bridge), which leads to Spree Island, and feast your eyes on treasures from around the world in the superb cluster of museums at Museumsinsel. After your culture fix, head to the Reichstag and watch the sunset from its famous glass dome.

8pm Indulge in a *Wiener Schnitzel* and top-notch people-watching at Borchardt in Mitte. After some bar hopping (try the gorgeous beer garden at Heinz Minki, the glam Anhalt and Freischimmer with its casual vibe), it's off to Watergate, one of Berlin's most sizzling clubs.

5am Soothe the ringing in your ears by quietly watching the sun rise over the river before going home.

Copenhagen

9am Start in Strøget, Copenhagen's famous pedestrian street, with a coffee and a Danish pastry (*wienerbrød*) in any of the numerous cafés. Check out the action in City Hall Square on your way to Dansk Design Center to see some seriously innovative Danish design.

1pm After a quick trip to Tivoli Gardens, head to Ida Davidsen for a lunch of *smørrebrød* (open sandwiches) and fjord prawns – you'll melt in front of the 250-strong selection of sandwiches.

3pm Walk across Knippelsbro, a wonderful Funkis-style bridge, to the island of Christianshavn, where you can hire a boat and explore this delightful place's historic canals. Later, enjoy a draught beer (*fadøl*) at an outdoor table at Nyhavn, followed by dinner at Restaurant Leonora Christine in Nyhavn's oldest building.

7pm Catch the Danish Royal Ballet at Det Kongelige Teater (Royal Theatre) and end your night by sampling a few cocktails at retro-style Barbarella, open until very late – or is that very early?

Istanbul

9am Start your day at Sultanahmet Parkı, where costumed juice sellers preen themselves for the full day of photography ahead (does my moustache look big in this?). Head to Aya Sofya, one of the world's great buildings, and marvel at the apparent lack of support for the enormous dome.

11am Walk along the ancient Roman road, Divan Yolu, to enter the Grand Bazaar from its southern end. As you meander through the glittering gold arcade, poke your head into the gorgeous pink Zincirli Han (Caravan Inn).

3pm Shop in the Grand Bazaar, or prepare your elbows and join the crush of locals in the ancient shopping district of Tahtakale.

7pm Make your way to İstiklal Caddesi, the city's 'main drag' and centre of its thriving eating, bar and club scene. The choices for dinner are endless, but some of our favourites are Badehane, the Soho Supper Club and 5 Kat.

Lisbon

8am Take your *pão* (bread) and *café com leite* (coffee with milk) standing at a Baixa café as the city's distinctive trams rumble through the tight grid of its 18th-century streets.

9am Hop on Tram No 28, which heads uphill past the Romanesque cathedral and through Alfama's labyrinthine hillside streets. Admire Castelo São Jorge as it looms into view, and marvel at the grand baroque monasteries, paid for with Brazilian gold.

10am Get off at Largo da Graça and head back down the hill, spending the rest of the day exploring all the places you've just passed. Enjoy a picnic lunch on the walls of the Castelo, followed by a nap in its orchard-like garden.

8pm Stroll down to the Miradouro Santa Catarina to watch the river, sky and city turn rosy, then purple. Sit down for beer and seafood at Cervejaria da Trindade before heading to the Barrio Alto district's clubs at midnight.

24 hours in the city

Paris

9am Stock up on fresh provisions at a *marché alimentaire* (street food market) before stopping for a *grand crème* (coffee with cream) and a *pain au chocolat* (chocolate croissant) at Ma Bourgogne in the scrumptious Place des Vosges.

12pm Head to the Île de la Cité and eschew Nôtre Dame in favour of the smaller, more delicate Ste-Chapelle. Before lunch somewhere on the Rue Montorgueil (a market street), window-shop at the boutiques of Rue Étienne Marcel.

3pm Rent a bike and play chicken with the traffic in the middle of Place de l'Étoile. For something tamer, make your way to the Musée Auguste Rodin and admire the sculptor's sublime *The Thinker*.

6pm Any corner café works for an *apéro* (sundowner), but since we recommend dinner at Juan et Juanita in Ménilmontant, head to the L'Autre Café and ask for their finest bottle of *Pastis 51*.

Rome

7am Arrive at St Peter's Basilica with the larks and marvel at Michelangelo's devastating *Pietà*, before tackling the treasure-filled hallways and galleries of the Vatican Museum. Your trek will end at the Sistine Chapel, home to Michelangelo's celebrated frescoes of the *Creation* and *Last Judgement*.

12pm Catch your breath over a leisurely lunch at Cul De Sac near Piazza Navona. If you dare, head to the piazza's Tre Scalini and ask for its most famous creation: a decadent concoction of chocolate *gelato*, huge chunks of chocolate and whipped cream.

2pm Walk off your indulgence at the Pantheon, before exploring the ruins of the Roman Forum and the iconic Colosseum.

8pm Trastevere is very beautiful at night, and has dozens of good restaurants. Have your post-dinner cappuccino or *aperitivo* on Piazza Santa Maria, and you'll enjoy the view not only of its basilica, but also of the people parading past.

Stockholm

8am Have a *lussekatt* (saffron bun) and coffee at Thelins Konditori in Kungsholmen. Make your way to Skeppsholmen to view Moderna Museet's world-class collection of modern art, sculpture and installations.

11pm Hop on the *tunnelbana* (metro) to Gamla Stan in time to watch the midday changing of the guards at Kungliga Slottet. Wander the cobbled streets of the old town, stopping to *fika* (have coffee and cake) in the city's oldest café, Sundbergs Konditori.

3pm Take in the 'time-travel' exhibit of Stockholm growth and culture at Stockholms Stadmuseum. Then catch the Katarinahissen lift to the top and enjoy the spectacular evening view.

7pm Dine at Eriks Gondolen atop Katrinahissen or try the *husmanskost* (traditional Swedish fare) at Östgötakällaren. Afterwards, join the enthusiastic locals at one of the bars in Södermalm, Stockholm's undisputed capital of alcohol consumption.

	Da	Du	Fr	Ge	Gr	It	Po	Sp	Sw	Tu
doctor	22	32	42	52	62	72	82	92	102	112
drinks	19	29	39	49	59	69	79	89	99	109

E

	Da	Du	Fr	Ge	Gr	It	Po	Sp	Sw	Tu
eating & drinking	18	28	38	48	58	68	78	88	98	108
email	15	25	36	45	56	65	75	85	95	105
emergencies	22	32	42	52	62	72	82	92	102	112
English (use of)	15	25	35	45	55	65	75	85	95	105
entertainment	20	30	40	50	60	70	80	90	100	110

F

	Da	Du	Fr	Ge	Gr	It	Po	Sp	Sw	Tu
festivals					8					
film (camera)	21	31	41	51					101	111
food & drink	18	28	38	48	58	68	78	88	98	108

G

	Da	Du	Fr	Ge	Gr	It	Po	Sp	Sw	Tu
gay venues	20	30	40	50	60	70	80	90	100	110
goodbyes	17	28	38	48	58	68	78	88	98	108
greetings	15	25	35	45	55	65	75	85	95	105

H

	Da	Du	Fr	Ge	Gr	It	Po	Sp	Sw	Tu
hotel	19	29	39	49	59	69	79	89	99	109

I

	Da	Du	Fr	Ge	Gr	It	Po	Sp	Sw	Tu
interests	18	28	38	48	58	68	78	88	98	108
introductions	15	25	35	45	55	65	75	85	95	105
invitations	17	27	37	47	57	67	77	87	97	107
Istanbul					119					

L

	Da	Du	Fr	Ge	Gr	It	Po	Sp	Sw	Tu
languages of Western Europe					5					
language difficulties	15	25	35	45	55	65	75	85	95	105
Lisbon					120					
luggage	20	30	40	50	60	70	80	90	100	110

Index

Index

Internal photographs p114 Red-light district, Amsterdam – Christian Aslund • p115 Acropolis Museum, Athens – Anders Blomqvist • p116 Gaudi's Temple of La Sagrada Familia, Barcelona – Neil Setchfield • p117 Reichstag dome interior, Berlin – Andrea Schulte-Peevers • p118 Nyhavn restaurants, Copenhagen – John Elk III • p119 Mystical Water Pipes and Tea Garden, Istanbul – Greg Elms • p120 Tram, Lisbon – Christopher Groenhout • p121 Sidewalk café, Paris – Lou Jones • p122 Outdoor dining near the Pantheon, Rome – Martin Moos • p123 Gold crown in front of Gamla Stan, Stockholm – Wayne Walton

What kind of traveller are you?

A. You're eating chicken for dinner *again* because it's the only word you know.

B. When no one understands what you say, you step closer and shout louder.

C. When the barman doesn't understand your order, you point frantically at the beer.

D. You're surrounded by locals, swapping jokes, email addresses and experiences – other travellers want to borrow your phrasebook or audio guide.

If you answered A, B, or C, you NEED Lonely Planet's language products ...

- **Lonely Planet Phrasebooks** – for every phrase you need in every language you want
- **Lonely Planet Language & Culture** – get behind the scenes of English as it's spoken around the world – learn and laugh
- **Lonely Planet Fast Talk & Fast Talk Audio** – essential phrases for short trips and weekends away – read, listen and talk like a local
- **Lonely Planet Small Talk** – 10 essential languages for city breaks
- **Lonely Planet Real Talk** – downloadable language audio guides from lonelyplanet.com to your MP3 player

... and this is why

- **Talk to everyone everywhere**
  Over 120 languages, more than any other publisher
- **The right words at the right time**
  Quick-reference colour sections, two-way dictionary, easy pronunciation, every possible subject – and audio to support it

Lonely Planet Offices

Australia
90 Maribyrnong St, Footscray,
Victoria 3011
☎ 03 8379 8000
fax 03 8379 8111
✉ talk2us@lonelyplanet.com.au

USA
150 Linden St, Oakland,
CA 94607
☎ 510 893 8555
fax 510 893 8572
✉ info@lonelyplanet.com

UK
72-82 Rosebery Ave,
London EC1R 4RW
☎ 020 7841 9000
fax 020 7841 9001
✉ go@lonelyplanet.co.uk

lonelyplanet.com